Watching Paint Dry

Watching Paint Dry

STORIES FROM THE TRADE

John Burbidge

Cover and text design: Jeff Wincapaw
Layout: Dana Kim-Wincapaw

Library of Congress Control Number: 2012934438

ISBN 978-0-9840210-0-0

To the painters

contents

author's note

First fact about paint: it's only one-thousandth of an inch thick when dry. But that one-thousandth of an inch protects and colorizes most of what humans construct on this planet, so what it lacks in depth it recovers in width, despite going largely unnoticed except by the people who put it there. The painters.

This book is for them. Dressed in white as they craft a backdrop to civilization, painters invite invisibility, smarting from the stigma of a simpleton occupation. "Just a dumb old painter" is how one of my bosses described himself, yet here he was running a successful business, keeping several people employed, performing a task that preserved and enhanced all the earthly resources that go into making buildings. I heard that same sense of unworthiness expressed by many other career painters, and it needled me. After fifteen years I'd yet to master all the nuances of painting, and I didn't get a sense I ever would. *Simple* is about the last word I would use to describe it.

This narrative starts at the beginning of my painting career and finishes at the end of it. In the middle is a procession of painters whose stories touched my life as the paint jobs that brought us together were completed. Some of these people are still painting, some are in jail, and some are dead from their own destructive doings. But wherever they are, aboveground or below, locked up or let out, to them I say this: *simple* is about the last word I would use to describe you.

college crooks

I showed up at 7 a.m. on my first morning as a college painter, bleary with a hangover but not worried. How hard could
it be? You stick a brush in front of your face and wave it
around all day. I yawned and plodded over to a trailer where
a group of guys stood.

Within three minutes I was lifting heavy extension ladders off the trailer with a partner named Dan and muscling
the unwieldy beasts into position against a house. A few
minutes later we'd bridged the gap between the ladders
with a long scaffold plank. Dan began floating across our
makeshift balance beam, bucket in one hand and brush in
the other, while I clutched a window sill and commented
about the cement sidewalk thirty feet below us. Dan just
shrugged as if to say, now is the time to decide if you want to

be a painter, pal, because this is what it's all about. Heights with your hands full.

··

My mother pushed me into painting. It's unfortunate that almost two decades later she ended up being the person most concerned that I was still struggling to get out of it, but I guess that's parenthood. No matter what happens it's your fault.

It all started in Minnesota during my first summer home from attending college in Montana. I was on the verge of going back to my high school job at an Arby's. The restaurant had offered me a raise, from $3.85 to $4 an hour, but my mom saw a newspaper ad for college-age painters, a job that paid $5 with a midsummer raise to $6. She "encouraged" me to apply so I could make as much spending money as possible for the next school year.

As I filled out the application, I would have laughed if you had told me I was signing up for the long haul. My mom would have laughed too, but she wasn't laughing twenty years later when trying to describe what her forty-one-year-old son did for a living. I overheard her once telling somebody I was a writer, without mentioning painting at all. I do write, but that's not what the person was asking.

This barefaced omission of my real work stung a bit, but I forgave her. She just wanted the same thing she wanted twenty years ago—a good job for her son. Whatever caused me to lose (or never find in the first place) any white-collar ambition was my own innovation. It likely had something to do with being raised upper middle class and then moving to Montana and wanting to reinvent myself as blue-collar gritty because Montana is a tough place. But such youthful fancy is not my mom's fault. And understand this much about a woman who grew up picking potatoes before school in North Dakota: embarrassed she might be, but not nearly enough to bail me out.

..

That summer with the college painters was a learning experience. Literally. The company required all rookies to attend ten weeks of classes, do weekly homework assignments in a workbook, and take a final test at the end that included a performance element—you actually had to show them you knew how to paint a window frame in the fastest possible time, or demonstrate the exact method of partnering up to paint siding quickly without using a sprayer, just one guy winging a roller and the other guy brushing the paint out with hummingbird-like speed. But they paid us for the class time and we got a $250 bonus if we passed the exam, so everybody took it seriously enough.

Bonuses were, in fact, the company's primary motivational tool, and they were constantly dangling them in front of us. First there was the speed bonus, enticing crews to blast through two or even three houses a week. Then there was the customer satisfaction bonus, based on the comment card each homeowner filled out after final inspection. The latter bonus, of course, was meant to counter the corners inevitably cut as a result of the former bonus.

It would be a logical theory, except that it's entirely possible to paint a house in a way that looks great the day you finish but that will actually leave everlasting scars. The comment card might read: "House looks great. Nice bunch of guys, and so fast!" and all the *Very Satisfied* fives would be circled, and the crew would earn the maximum bonus. But underneath that crisp new paint job, devils lurked, already planning their ascent to the surface. Of course, by the time those devils raised hell the collegiate minions who had spawned them would be long gone from the trade.

..

The crew I worked on didn't screw people. We gave good paint jobs, as did most of the company's fourteen crews in the Twin Cities area. But without question there were two or three rogue outfits every summer who left behind a trail of unsuspecting, wronged homeowners, nice people who were trying to help college kids pay for their education and who got screwed as a result.

Oh, but the company was smart. They were so smart, they had figured out a way to deal with this dirty little secret and even turn it to their advantage, a way to put all customers' minds at ease about hiring unaccountable, temporary college painters. What they came up with was the "100% guaranteed paint job."

Five years came standard. Ten years could be purchased—even a *lifetime* guarantee on the paint job was available. No questions asked: if your paint job fails, we will come back and fix it free of charge. Do you see other companies willing to stand behind their paint jobs like that? No, we offer the only written guarantee in the business. Forget about the rotating crop of college students; what we really are is a growing company with franchises all over the Midwest and $20 million a year in sales. We are not fly-by-nighters, and our guarantee proves it.

In their fifteenth year of business with guarantee problems up the wazoo when I started, the company had no choice but to keep several "guarantee crews" racing around the city, fixing rotten paint jobs. It was during my second summer with the college painters that I became the foreman of a guarantee crew, and it was that summer I learned exactly how much damage can be done with the soft bristles of a paint brush.

..

Foremen earned $10 an hour plus bonuses, pretty good for the mid-1980s. We were required to take another round of classes that focused more on the business side of painting, such as how to manage employees, schedule jobs, collect payment, and maintain positive customer relations. That last one proved almost impossible for those of us assigned to lead guarantee crews. Most customers despised us before we even showed up.

On the final day of orientation, the regional supervisor handed me a stack of work orders as thick as a bible. "Just call a few people every night when you get home and tell them you're coming the next day." He nodded at the stack of orders. "You'll burn through that pretty quick. We'll give you more when you run out."

That evening I picked up the phone and started making calls, doing my best to sound confident and disguise my rumbling gut. You got a paint problem? Well, have no fear, because help is on the way.

..

The first house in my stack of work orders was owned by a retired military guy who'd purchased a lifetime guarantee on his paint job ten years ago. One side of the house now cracked and peeled every year. He was waiting for us in his driveway when we pulled up at precisely 8 a.m. The look on his face said he appreciated punctuality.

"You guys come every summer and repaint it, but it keeps cracking," he said as he showed me the problem area.

"What's going on is you have old oil-based paint underneath the latex." I picked off a peeling piece and snapped it apart, exactly like my training manual told me to do. "See how brittle that is? Latex alone would never do that, because latex is flexible, like a thin coat of rubber. But if you have oil paint underneath, it can turn brittle and crack right through the latex."

"You guys tell me the same thing every year," he said. "But nobody will ever tell me why you put the latex on top of the oil in the *first* place, if this is what happens."

"It doesn't happen all the time, only in rare instances." The training manual emphasized that the benefits of modern latex far outweighed the occasional odd reaction with the old coat of oil, but I doubted he wanted to hear that, so I took an alternate route. "Notice how it only happens on the south side of your house? The extreme exposure to the sun probably has a lot to do with it." I'd been instructed to always raise the issue of the sun on any south-side problems (as opposed to north-side problems, which we blamed on a lack of said sun—that is, it's always damp over there).

The guy laughed and folded his arms. "Well, as long as you keep coming back and fixing it, I guess I don't care." He seemed perversely happy to be taking full advantage of a guarantee, despite the south side of his house looking like baked shit after so many recoats. But his relaxed attitude helped ease me into my new life as a guarantee-crew leader. This isn't so bad, I thought: just smile and recite the lines. You can do this.

..

The next house shook me awake. We showed up after lunch, and an older lady met us in the driveway. She was wearing a blue robe and frowning.

"This is all new siding," she said, leading us to the nearest part of the house. "I had it put on last summer, and I hired you college guys to paint it." She sounded disgusted with the decision. "Now look at this. Why is it doing this?"

She pointed to her new six-inch lapboard wood siding, beautiful except for the proliferation of quarter-sized, domelike bubbles growing in the blue paint. I picked at one of the blisters with my fingernail; it broke open, then deflated slightly.

"Something is trying to break through the paint," I said with authority. "It's either moisture from inside the house, or some type of gas from the wood."

"Gas?"

"Sometimes new boards have gas pockets in them, and the gas tries to come out after it's painted. It's a very rare problem. It almost never happens."

She scowled. It wasn't rare to her. "Well, what are you going to do about it?"

"All we can really do at this point is scrape the bubbles off, prime the bare wood underneath, and repaint it."

"But how's that going to look? Won't it leave a mark?"

You're damn right it will leave a mark, I thought, but I forged ahead with my spiel. "We'll also hammer in some of these wedge-vents underneath the siding so the house can release moisture better." I held up the small plastic wedge-vent I'd been instructed to carry in my pocket for just such occurrences.

She took the wedge-vent and turned it over in her fingers. "Why didn't you guys put these in the first time?"

"Not all houses require it, only those that have a problem venting moisture. But like I said, it could be gas in the wood, and wedge-vents probably wouldn't have prevented that anyway, so . . . "

She shook her head in disbelief. She was clearly not rich, and spending a big chunk of money on her house had likely caused tangible sacrifices in other areas of her life. "Well, all I know is I don't want a bunch of ugly craters all over my new siding."

Craters were exactly what she was going to get, so I decided to slow things down. "Let me call my boss," I said. "Can I use your phone?"

She nodded, looking a tad relieved, and pointed me toward the kitchen door.

"Scrape it, prime it, and paint it," he said. "You gotta move on."

"It's not going to look very good."

"There's nothing we can do about that."

"How about using some spackle? We could smooth the craters out a bit, sand them down . . ."

"It would take way too long, and it still wouldn't look that good. Just scrape it, prime it, and paint it. And use the wedge-vents so it hopefully doesn't keep happening."

"But—"

"Look," he said, "sometimes stuff happens due to uncontrollable variables like this. All you can do is scrape it, prime it, paint it, and move on. From the street it won't even be noticeable."

Back outside I told the lady what my boss said, including the line about uncontrollable variables. Her face sagged into her robe. She went inside.

At the end of the day I took her out to the street for a look. "You can't even tell from here," I said, but she only sniffed. She didn't live in the street, she lived in the house, and she would see those ugly craters every day.

..

As disturbing as that first day was, my second day as a guarantee-crew leader established, without a doubt, the bleak challenge I faced that summer.

The victim this time was a beautiful, three-story Victorian, elegantly crafted with intricate gables and covered porches. It was situated peacefully, far back from the street, surrounded by a lush lawn and mature trees. The owners were standing in the driveway when we pulled in—"we" meaning me and Eric, the only guy I was in charge of. My boss had promised me another guy but didn't say when. Guarantee crews were small because the jobs were often quick fixes, and more guys meant more standing around.

This one didn't have the feel of a quick fix. On the phone the night before, I'd talked to a woman who spoke in a clipped, emotionless tone. In the background I'd heard an angry husband. Now he strode toward us with a hostile gait that kicked my heart up. He stared with contempt at my little red Dodge Colt, which I'd had fitted with a custom trailer hitch to pull one of the company's bright red paint trailers stacked high with ladders. The trailer dwarfed the car, and the whole entourage looked a little ridiculous. It certainly didn't look like the rig of a professional painter, like the one he wished he'd hired.

His wife stood back while he yelled and cussed. He appeared to be on his way to work, judging by his pressed clothes, but he'd probably stayed until we showed up so he could have his moment of rage. He called us "college crooks" and said he was going to sue if we didn't figure out what was wrong and fix it. The paint on all his beautiful beamed eaves was shredding like tissue paper—why? He waved his arms in the air when he asked the question, but I didn't answer because he didn't want an explanation. I stood and took it while Eric scuttled back to the trailer and started unloading equipment.

Finally, the guy got in his expensive car, slammed the door, and zoomed off.

"I'm sorry," his wife said. She was wearing a loose shirt that might have been maternity.

"That's okay."

"We just bought this house last year, and . . ."

"Uh-huh." Their dream house, and it didn't come cheap. "Well, let's go take a look."

We walked over to the house, which was painted white except for dark green shutters. The woman pointed up at the porch ceiling and some nearby eaves where the white paint was releasing itself from the wood in obscene swaths of scaly flakes, as if the house had psoriasis. No homeowner could enjoy a glass of lemonade on that porch with such an unsightly mess hanging over their head.

I climbed onto the porch railing and rubbed my finger over a small section of the ceiling. The paint crumbled off with no resistance. I wiped my finger against the surface underneath the flaking paint. Then I climbed down and held it up for her to see. It was smudged white. "Chalking," I said.

"Chalking?"

"Sometimes old paint jobs get a chalky residue built up on them. It attracts the dirt in the air, pollutants you can't even see, pollen, all kinds of stuff. It creates an unstable layer, and paint won't stick to it."

"Oh." She took in a breath. "Well, what can be done about it?"

We both knew the answer to that: the house can be washed *before* it gets painted. Jesus Christ.

"Let me call my boss," I said. She nodded and led me inside.

"Scrape it, prime it, and paint it."

"But it looks—"

"I know what it looks like. . . . I already went out there to talk to them." He paused, seeming unsure of how much company culpability he should admit. Then he relented, almost under his breath. "It didn't get washed properly is what happened. The assholes on that crew left behind a lot of fucked-up jobs that summer. Now we're dealing with the aftermath." He sounded like he'd love to track them down, step on their throats, and take back all the bonus money they'd scammed during their lark as painters.

"It's going to take a long time," I said, letting him know my own production bonus was now in danger because the company gave me a skimpy average of eight man-hours per job—a half day for me and Eric—and had made it clear I was not to let homeowners intimidate me into doing more work than was necessary.

"That's okay," he said, "just do what you have to do. I won't count the extra time against your average."

"Shouldn't we at least wash it?"

He sighed. "It won't really do much good at this point because the problem is underneath. But yeah, go ahead and wash it. Then scrape it, prime it, and paint it. It's all we can do, short of sandblasting, and we're not doing that."

Back outside I smiled at the woman. "My boss told me to take as long as necessary to fix the problem."

She looked relieved. "What are you going to do?"

"Wash the problem areas, scrape off the loose paint, prime it, and repaint."

"Oh . . ." she said, her worry returning. "But won't it just keep happening in other areas where it's not coming off yet?"

I chose not to lie. "It might. But if it does, we'll come back and fix it."

She sighed. "All right." I saw a peculiar brand of confusion cross her face as she turned away. Like many people I would encounter in the next few months, she'd been ambushed by painting, never giving it much thought until it snuck up behind and whacked her on the head.

..

That summer on the guarantee crew I learned about more paint problems than I ever would have imagined existed. I learned about customer service the hard way, with every homeowner predisposed to hate me. I successfully managed an employee and created a productive partnership between us. I worked my mind and body to exhaustion but received little satisfaction for a job well done. Those jobs were not well done. They were a bleeding mess, and all we could do was slap on a few Band-Aids.

But my sympathy grew for the people who'd been ill-treated, and I yearned to immerse myself in happy customers, satisfied customers, and houses properly protected by a quality paint job, not this fraudulent B.S. I was witnessing job after job. I wanted to start my own painting company—be a real painter—and make sure things got done right. Because painting, simple as it had seemed on the surface, was actually kind of important.

2

---

college craftsmen

The notion of starting my own painting company did not get immediately realized. The summer following my indoctrination on the guarantee crew, I stayed in Montana after classes let out and looked for painting work. Through a friend, I hooked up with a property management company that oversaw a twenty-building apartment complex where all the windows were peeling. The windows came in two sizes, big and small, and every day I went from big window to small window to big window to small window, scraping off the peeling paint, priming, and painting.

In terms of variety, the job was a big step back from the guarantee crew. Nonetheless, I discovered that the low-stress monotony of painting the same two windows all day every day did not bother me. I listened to cassette tapes on a Sony Walkman and dreamed of the next weekend's back-packing trip or peak climb.

As much as I enjoyed the Zen of painting windows, the job only paid $5 an hour—half what I'd been making the previous year as a guarantee-crew leader—and as the following summer neared, my mom made it clear how she felt about my diminished contribution to my school expenses. I wasn't too crazy about it either. I knew there was money to be made painting—I just had to figure out how to get it. I thought about that "help a kid pay for college" shtick and how it worked wonders for the company in Minneapolis. Why reinvent the roller?

And that's how the College Craftsmen were born.

..

When you look back on the summers of your life, one or two probably stand out for the experiences you had and the people you had them with. For me, the year of the College Craftsmen became such a summer. I was partnered with a great friend, we made good money, and we had plenty of time off to play around in the mountains as well. But the fun didn't come without a stiff painting lesson: sometimes you fuck up a house. And when you fuck up a house, you can smile and be clean-cut and articulate and everything most painters aren't—but you can't overcome the emotional attachment people have for their houses. They'll side with the house every time. They'll scream at you on the house's behalf.

The summer started innocuously enough. My friend Barry and I were on the cusp of our senior year. We were fraternity brothers: I'd just finished a stint as president, and Barry had just finished a term as treasurer. The weight of responsibility was off our shoulders, and we were feeling ready to do something different. Barry owned a truck, and his dad had a few ladders he could lend us. Why not start a painting company?

So we did. A legitimate one, with bonding and insurance. And it was successful right away. We generated almost all our business by delivering flyers in nice neighborhoods. We gave people good paint jobs and left behind a string of happy homeowners. Maybe we got cocky, I don't know, but some disasters of our own creation lurked ahead that summer.

..

Our first slipup seemed bad initially but turned out to be just a mild prelude. We were painting the house of a University of Montana economics professor. On a midweek whim—the only one that got the better of us all summer—we left the job half done and went to climb a mountain. Three days in the backcountry proved to be exactly the refresher we needed, and we returned to Missoula exalted. Our elation evaporated, though, when we checked the messages on Barry's answering machine.

"I don't know where you guys are, but you better get over here fast." The professor's tone was agitated, and the message was two days old. Shit.

We jumped in Barry's truck and raced to the house. The professor was gone, but we could see why he was pissed. About ten storm windows we'd left leaning against the house had blown over and lay flat on the lawn. Nothing appeared broken, though, so maybe the guy was overreacting. A bit sheepishly we started picking the windows up.

"Uh-oh," Barry said. He pointed at the seared, dead grass underneath each pane of glass, where the lawn had been branded like a cow on the Storm Window Ranch.

It was the same under every one. We couldn't believe grass could die so quickly and completely like that, but it was white-brown burned in neat squares right down the row. Obviously, the sun shining through the glass had done it. Surely the professor had lifted them up and seen what was going on; he must have decided to leave them down on purpose so we could experience the full impact of our irresponsibility.

He never said anything about it, though, until the day of final inspection. He walked around the house and pointed out a couple spots he wanted touched up, but overall the job looked great and he was pleased. The last thing he did was glance down at the latticed lawn and slide his foot over some dead grass. "I assume this will grow back," he said, and he handed us our check.

Barry and I gave him a relieved look and shook his hand: lesson learned, guy, and thanks. You are a true teacher.

..

So we got off easy on that one. We would not be so lucky, though, later in the summer, when two women asked us to strip for them.

Strip their house, of course. They owned a nice rambler north of Missoula in an upscale area we had hit hard with flyers. The house's beautiful redwood siding had been stained; unfortunately, somebody had then applied a thick coat of clear varnish on top of the stain. The sun had burned through that clear coat the same way it had burned through the professor's storm windows, and now the varnish was cracking and peeling in a way painters call "alligatoring," which pretty much describes how it looks.

"Can you strip this varnish off and restain the siding?" one of the women asked. Her partner stood a little behind her to the side.

Barry and I looked at each other. The women had caught us amid the only real lull in work we had experienced that summer, and we were getting desperate.

"I think you should consider having us sand it down and paint it," I said. "It would look great." And it would be a hell of a lot easier.

She shook her head. "I don't want it painted. It's redwood, and I want it stained natural. That varnish never should have been put on there in the first place. We didn't do it—the previous owners did."

I nodded. Previous owners do a lot of boneheaded things with paint.

"So can you do it?"

"Uh . . . yeah, we can do it," I said, and we all signed the contract.

Barry and I went straight to the paint store and asked the manager for advice. "Walk away from it," he said grimly, putting his hands flat on the counter.

We were stunned. The manager liked nothing more than pushing his products on us, so this was a genuine setback.

"I'm serious. Walk away from it."

But we were determined, so he sighed and started showing us strippers in various levels of toxicity, the stronger the better, of course, while still considering other factors, such as the amount of plant life you'll be working around. We settled on a medium-strength stripper, along with thick rubber gloves and goggles. Then we set out to make a giant stinking mess of everything.

..

"I don't want it painted."

"I'm just saying—"

"I don't *care* what you're saying. *I don't want it painted.*" She was crying. Her partner stood behind her, arms folded, a sad frown on her face.

It was a week later, and we were standing in the front yard looking at the house. The house, oh my God, the poor house. We were on our third stripper now, nothing was working, and the redwood siding was desecrated with streaky black patches about 100 square feet in size, half varnish-on and half varnish-off, the wood grooved and damaged from where we'd scraped too hard in pure frustration. Note to self: next time experiment on the *back* of the house, you freaking idiot.

Nonetheless, I couldn't understand why she was so opposed to paint. It will look beautiful, I said. Paint protects better than stain anyway, I told her. You can pick any color you want, any combination, and I guarantee you we will make your house look so awesome you'll be thrilled, you'll love it. Lady! Listen to me! You're going to love it!

But she ignored my pleas, and after screaming that we better figure out a way to "fix" her house, she and her partner went inside and slammed the door.

Thoroughly discouraged, Barry and I went back to the paint store and laid ourselves bare before the manager. We were fucked. Did he have any idea at all for how we could get out of this disaster?

After a moment's hesitation, the manager reached under the counter and pulled out a business card. He pushed it toward us like a wizard divulging a secret that was equal parts salvation and damnation.

"Call this guy."

I looked at the card. "Who's this?"

"Big contractor. He tackles a lot of tough jobs. Give him a call. He might be able to sandblast it or something."

I called the contractor that night and left a message, explaining the situation. He called back immediately—screening his calls, never a great sign—and asked for the address.

"I'll go take a look." He hung up.

We waited to hear back from him but never did. But we never heard from the women, either, nor did we initiate contact. Later that summer, though, our curiosity prevailed and we took a surreptitious drive past their house. The freshly stained redwood looked gorgeous, and we were elated. Damn, we said, whoever that guy is, he sure saved our asses. He tackles tough jobs, just like the manager told us.

I didn't know it then, but years later I would repay "that guy" by tackling the toughest, most dangerous paint job of my life for him, dangling from climbing ropes to spray the inside of a roaring, pulsing pulp mill—a job much more challenging than that redwood, which was so easy he didn't even remember it.

3

fallers and fakers

Thinking of the first time I almost fell to my death still tightens up my insides more than twenty years later. It happened during my first summer as a college painter in Minneapolis. The crew leader had instructed me to take down two small shutters that adorned a peak vent near the top of a tall house. I set up a fully extended thirty-six-foot ladder, but I still had to perch on the second-to-last rung to reach the shutters, keeping my weight pressed against the house so I wouldn't pitch off backward.

With my left hand I pinched the thin trim of the peak vent to hold myself in; with my right hand I slowly turned a screwdriver to loosen the first shutter. I managed to get all four rusty screws out, but the shutter remained stuck in place because I couldn't get any leverage from my precarious stance. Finally, I jammed the screwdriver behind the shutter and pried, hoping for any sort of separation.

What I got was a bat to the face.

The madly flapping creature exploded from its roost, bounced off my cheek, then grazed my ear before escaping.

I wobbled, and for an instant I felt my center of gravity collapse back into space, where waited a three-story plunge to the driveway. Fingers fired with adrenaline, I dropped the screwdriver, snatched the edge of the peak vent, and pulled myself in.

Slowly, I climbed down the ladder, both hands clutching the rungs and my chest still shaking. For such a surprise, it made perfect sense: bats live behind shutters. I just never really thought about it before.

..

Despite that near fall and others I've had over the years, I do not consider myself an accident-prone painter. Knock on wood siding, but I believe an occasional near fall demonstrates a fine-tuned sense of balance and respect for gravity. I have, however, worked with a few accident-prone painters, and their failed circus acts left a lasting impression. I've seen stupid ladder tricks result in broken ankles and injured backs; I've watched a fully extended man-lift tip over and pound its shocked occupant into the ground with the greatest of ease. But one fellow stands out in my mind as the most accident-prone painter I ever met: Randall.

I worked for Randall after dropping out of college. The

College Craftsmen had folded the year before, and my painting partner Barry had graduated and taken a position in Seattle as a sales rep for John Deere. Most of my other college friends similarly disbanded to various U.S. population centers in search of their first real jobs.

I wanted to stay in Montana and live amongst the mountains, though, so I needed to earn some sort of a living, my parents having understandably withdrawn their support after my school campaign ended without a degree (a form of merit I had come to view as rather soft, which is the only explanation I can conjure for quitting when I was just four classes and an internship short of being done). Barry's dad had reclaimed the ladders he'd lent us, so I wasn't in a position to go solo, and I didn't really want to be tied down that much anyway. I'd seen Randall's company trucks around town, with his phone number painted on the side, so one day I called him and asked for work. He needed help and that was that.

Randall and I hit it off right away. When I showed up the first day in my red Volkswagen van, he smiled broadly and insisted I give him a tour of the rig, which I had decked out for extended rock-climbing road trips. He asked me a lot of questions about climbing, and he told me about his own passion, windsurfing, sounding as though he'd wanted for a long time an employee who grasped the allure of exciting outdoor sports. He showed himself to be quick-witted and conversational, and he seemed successful, based on the fleet of smartly decorated company vehicles he owned and the full-page ad he ran in the Yellow Pages. He also had a big fancy shop behind his house on acreage just outside of town. I was certain I'd hooked up with a guy making a good living off painting, somebody I could learn from.

The crew, however, told a different story. They said Randall was $80,000 in debt to the IRS because he'd been busted for paying employees under the table. According to the crew, Randall was in danger of losing the company. Apparently, it was a company his father had bequeathed, and the crew members spewed about Randall that particular brand of contempt reserved for those who destroy what their father has built.

In fact, as the newest employee, I was immediately privy to all the slam-Randall gossip as the crew rushed to get me on their side before Randall got me on his. They told me Randall was a space cadet whose instructions had to be ignored if any job was to be done right. They told me Randall was a lazy fuck who just drove around in the van all day or snuck off to Oregon unannounced on one of his mysterious "windsurfing" trips, which everybody speculated were actually clandestine trysts with little boys in Portland because Randall was far too klutzy to windsurf. Then they asked me if I'd heard about his accidents—*No? Oh, man.* Then they'd tell me about his accidents, the exact number of which was difficult to determine but three or four of which had resulted in hospital stays. The accident everybody seemed most excited about had happened when Randall fell from a high scaffold setup and got bounced back and forth pachinko-style between the support bars all the way to the ground. He got beat up pretty badly, but man, was it funny to watch.

I listened but didn't jump to conclusions. Maybe Randall was having a hard time managing his business, but the crew members sounded to me like bitter followers who would never have the guts to run their own companies. Randall was a good guy. He *did* know how to paint; he'd taught me a lot already, including how to rapidly stain a huge stack of boards by feeding them through a machine he'd invented and built himself. And of course he knew how to wind-surf; he'd shown me all his equipment and talked about it at length—he just didn't bother explaining it to these idiots because they didn't understand windsurfing, whereas I did. There was nothing wrong with Randall, and some of these crew members had only to look in the mirror if they wanted to see ineptitude and stupidity.

Eventually, though, Randall did do something so unwise it made me wonder about him. He'd landed a big contract to paint boxcars for a railroad company. First, the filthy boxcars had to be "degreased," which meant spraying them with a powerful solvent and then power-washing it off. To accomplish this, Randall purchased a fifty-five-gallon drum of the solvent, brought it out to the rail yard, and instructed the crew to unload it from his truck. He commented about how expensive the stuff was, then wondered aloud how he was going to get it from the drum into the sprayer without spilling any of the spendy stuff on the ground. Oh wait, he said, I have an idea.

He rummaged around in the paint van and produced a piece of clear plastic hose. He stuck one end of the hose into the drum, put the other end in his mouth, and sucked hard.

His siphon system worked fabulously, but he didn't get his lips off the hose in time and an instant later he fell to the ground, screaming. The solvent was a real flesh eater, and he'd just ingested a mouthful. Next stop: the emergency room.

Randall was laid up at home for a couple of weeks after that. I decided to quit the crew to go spend a few months working at a fish cannery in Alaska, and I saw him only once before I left. At the end of my last day, he dragged himself out of his house and waved for me to stop as I drove down his driveway from the shop.

"Hey," he said in a raspy whisper. "How's it going?"

"Good. The question is, how are you?"

"I'm all right. I just wanted to say thanks, and have a good time in Alaska."

I nodded. "Thanks. I'll give you a call if I need work when I get back."

"Do that," he said, and we shook hands. Then he got to the point. "Hey, you wouldn't happen to have any painkillers, would you? I ran out, and I'm really hurting." He looked down sheepishly, knowing it was bad form for a boss to mooch from his employees. His hoarse, croaking voice made the request sound even more pathetic.

I did not have any painkillers, though, so I couldn't help him. He thanked me anyway and, after giving my van a final pat with the butt of his palm, shuffled back toward the house.

..

That fall, after I returned from Alaska, I ran into one of the crew members, James, in a bar downtown. I asked him if he was still working for Randall.

"Randall?" He gave me a strange look. "Randall's done, man."

"Done?"

"He's done. Didn't you hear about his accident?"

"You mean swallowing the solvent?"

"No, not that, man. His big accident. The one that happened later." Thrilled to have found somebody who hadn't heard, James eagerly filled me in. Randall had taken a gigantic ladder fall and been laid up for months. He'd had several surgeries and was now doing physical therapy, but the doctors had told him he would never regain full use of his arms.

"He's done as a painter," James said. "He's got all these braces and shit."

"How did he fall?"

"Well, that's the thing," James said, leaning toward me. "People think he staged it."

"Staged it?"

"Everybody thinks he did it on purpose."

"Why would he do that?"

James rolled his eyes. "So he wouldn't have to pay all those *back taxes*, man. There's a law that says if you get hurt and can't work anymore, you don't have to pay any back taxes you owe. The IRS forgives the debt, and Randall gets to collect disability the rest of his life. See," he said, leaning close again, "it was the only way out for him. He staged the accident on purpose."

I tried to gauge how much of James's story to believe. He wasn't the most vicious gossiper on the crew, but he was far from a nonparticipant. "So do you think he's faking his injuries too?"

James's face grew studied. "I'm not sure. Some people think so. He still goes out to Oregon on his little trips, and I've heard he still windsurfs out there." James didn't seem to wonder how Randall had been transformed from an incompetent idiot who couldn't windsurf into a calculating genius who could.

"Did you see the actual fall?"

James averted his eyes in disappointment. "I didn't, but a couple of the other guys did. They say he was way up on an extension ladder and just standing there, then he crouched like he was getting ready to jump—and then he did. Onto a cement slab. They swear it looked like he jumped on purpose."

I didn't respond, and James sensed I was doubting the credibility of the witnesses. "Normally, I wouldn't believe them," he said. "But I asked Randall myself one day."

"What did he say?"

"He didn't say anything, but the look on his face sure changed. Like he was shocked that I even said it—like he was amazed I had figured it out." He nodded. "That was all the proof I needed. He was busted and he knew it."

I didn't know what to think. Randall was a plotter and a planner. I'd seen it in the way he ran his business. He might have jumped to escape his money troubles, and he might have been faking his injuries, windsurfing incognito in

Oregon then acting like an invalid at home. As much as I liked him, I couldn't put it past him.

..

I got the chance to make up my own mind a year later. I came across Randall in a bar where he was drinking beer and playing pool. He was shooting with one arm; the other arm was supported by metal stays that ran from his neck and shoulders down to his hand, where a hinged claw opened and closed like a weak vending-machine crane that picks up prizes. He walked around the pool table with a distinct limp, and even though he'd always been skinny, he now was sickly thin.

Of course, I didn't ask Randall if he'd staged the accident, but as I talked to him I started to understand the heavy fine the fall had levied on his senses. He came across as only a fragile scrap of the Randall I'd known: slow to move, which could be expected, but also slow of mind, which saddened me because I used to really enjoy talking to him. Maybe the rumors were true; maybe he had staged the accident to avoid taxes and set himself up for disability payments. But Randall hadn't gotten away with anything, that much I knew. The pavement flat refused to play along.

4

union busters

Picture a tall, skinny painter about fifty years old. He's wearing bright red earmuffs—even though it's July—and pedaling a ten-speed bike down a dormitory hallway. You probably wouldn't pick him as the guy who busted the painters' union in Montana. I wouldn't have either until I saw him do it.

I first encountered Gene the day I showed up at the University of Montana's housing department to take a painting test. Paint this window, he said gruffly, and then stood back with his arms folded. I was nervous, wanting to land a dream job—in this case a union position that paid $16.25 an hour and only required me to work in the summer. The high wage meant that after being laid off in the fall I would qualify for maximum unemployment compensation, allowing me to spend most of the winter taking road trips south to rock climb, an obsession I'd acquired during college. I'd been bumping around between different painting gigs since my former accident-prone boss Randall had gone down in pain, but at twenty six years old I wanted something more reliable and professional. A respectable union position as a painter with the university sounded absolutely perfect, and this painting test was my chance to get it.

After painting the window I leaned in close to check all angles, making sure everything looked perfect. Then I straightened up, ready to field praise.

"You've got paint in your hair."

I felt my head—sticky. It must have happened when I leaned in close. I looked at the window and saw hair prints on the sash. Damn. I tried to feather them out, but the paint was already setting up and my brush left drag marks. The window was fucked, and there was nothing I could do about it now. Nor about the paint in my hair.

Gene shook his head, but his mouth hid a smile. "I suppose you'll do," he said, and thus began the most influential painting relationship of my life.

..

Starting day one of my first summer in his department, Gene began training me in his own methods. He demanded perfection from all his painters, often making crew members redo their work, but in me he had found somebody whose first effort consistently met his standards, and he appreciated that balance of physical and mental coordination that sometimes seems so strangely absent in the painting world. I don't know why he wanted to help me take my skills to the next level—or, for that matter, why he demanded perfection in dorm painting—but I'd guess he was simply bored. Twenty years as a maintenance painter for the university had left him little choice but to invent his own challenges.

With a summer crew of a dozen painters, Gene would lead a systematic attack on the inside of whatever dormitory he'd been told to paint. That first summer we did eleven-story Jesse Hall. We started on the eleventh floor and tackled three floors at a time, performing the same steps over and over and over again. Each floor was identical to the one above and below, each room indistinguishable from the room next door. The only thing that varied was the view out the windows.

On a certain level it was monotonous, but the union-negotiated benefits were almost impossible to find in the painting world: first of all a regular schedule, 7:30 a.m. to 4:00 p.m. every day, with two ten-minute breaks and a thirty-minute lunch; then a paid holiday, the Fourth of July; and, of course, the $16.25 hourly wage. The full-time university painters like Gene actually earned $12.70 an hour plus benefits; the temporary summer painters were compensated an extra $3.55 an hour because they didn't get benefits. The painters' union had stubbornly negotiated this compensation for the temporaries, and the university had agreed to it rather than risk a labor dispute.

The money all equaled out in the end, of course, but I noticed early on that the subject of our hourly wages brought a scowl to Gene's face. The university seemed to have an informal policy of hiring half college students and half professional painters for the summer crew, and Gene ended up training a bunch of rookies every summer while getting paid what seemed like less per hour for the privilege. Meanwhile, the union loved the rookies because it got to collect a $350 initiation fee from each one, garnishing it straight off the first paycheck. This was in addition to everybody's normal monthly fee of $80. "And what do we get for it?" Gene would ask when the subject came up. "I'll tell you what. Once every two years Vince Ames drives over here from Great Falls and spends an hour rubber-stamping our contract renewal with the university. Then he goes back to Great Falls, and we don't see him again for two years."

One day Gene added up all the union dues and fees the crew had paid over the course of two years. When he finished, he announced that Vince Ames and the union were making $10,000 an hour off us.

"Holy Christ," he said to himself. "You're kidding."

He held up the clipboard and stared at it wide-eyed, a move he sometimes employed when he wanted to emphasize a point about our painting progress. Then he shook his head and muttered, "What a load of crap."

..

June 17, 1994: the day of O.J.'s "last run" in the white Bronco with his buddy Fred Cowlings. Is there anybody in America who didn't talk about O.J. at work the next day? We on the dorm crew did. We talked about O.J. all summer long, and we were still talking about O.J. the following summer as his murder trial careened toward its conclusion, a country's collective attention held hostage. I was thirty years old that summer of 1995, working my fifth straight season on the dorm crew. The money was good and I only wanted to keep rolling with it, but it was all about to end.

"Of course he did it, you moron," Loni said, and the breakroom hushed. It was unusual to be ducking one of Loni's bitch-from-hell outbursts on the first day back, but we had O.J. to thank for that.

"Oh, *I'm* a moron?" Rip laughed. "Okay, Loni. Whatever."

"You are a moron, Rip. How do you expect to be a lawyer when you can't see the most obvious truth in front of your face?"

"Oh please, Loni, tell me how to be a lawyer." Rip laughed again.

"I could tell you a few things if you'd listen, but you won't." Rip's implication that she was the real moron infuriated Loni, who considered herself his intellectual superior in every way. Could Rip complete a Sunday crossword puzzle in minutes? Did he have an M.F.A. in creative writing? Did he read the *New Yorker* and honestly enjoy it? Loni laid claim to all three.

But to Rip she was just a fifty-year-old painter who was getting big around the middle. "Whatever, Loni," he said again, folding his muscled arms and maintaining a perfect beach-boy smile. A former standout University of Montana Grizzly football player, he still carried the confidence of that celebrity. Now he was attending law school at Gonzaga, in Spokane, Washington, firmly on the road to success. Summers he spent in Missoula, his hometown, so he could work on the dorm crew and make $16.25 an hour.

But Loni had been a looker back in her day, and she carried enduring confidence too. Right now she seemed ready to explode from her seat and slap Rip, but at that moment Gene walked in. He smelled burnt emotions and stopped, looking around. The room was silent, and Loni stayed still. Finally, Gene walked to the head of the table and took his seat. The summer was about to begin.

..

"As I suppose you've all heard by now," Gene said, "I've filed a petition to withdraw all university painters from the painters' union."

We'd heard. The union had been barraging us with propaganda all spring, and a stay-in-or-get-out vote was set for August. The union was desperate because the university system painters were the last bastion of the organization in Montana. We were a small group—only fourteen full-time guys statewide, in addition to about fifty temporary painters hired on every summer—but it was enough to keep the union alive in Montana. Gene's petition had spurred the union brass into a full-on publicity campaign aimed at instilling fear in us and discrediting Gene.

"And if you want to talk to me about the union business after work, fine," Gene said. "But I can't talk about it at work—that's one of the rules. So I don't want any discussion of union business in the breakroom. This is where we come to relax."

His proclamation about relaxing segued into a tense silence. Nobody could relax when Loni's fuse was lit, but worse than that was the matter of Billy Ames—the son of Vince Ames, the union boss—sitting in the room with us.

Billy was a student at the university, and this was his third summer on the crew. Of course he'd heard grumbling about the union before, but Gene's filing of a petition to decertify was a direct attack against Billy's family. I'd thought he might quit to avoid the awkward situation of working for Gene, but here he was on the first morning, looking grim but determined to defend the Ames's honor. Normally, our return to dorm painting was an enjoyable reunion of sorts, but not this year.

"And no politics in the breakroom," Gene said, continuing with his first-day-of-class speech. "That's not relaxing either." He nodded his head slightly left at a painter named Tom, a self-described redneck who listened to Rush Limbaugh all day on his headphones and regularly agreed out loud, driving everybody nuts. The room did relax a tad at Tom's expense as we all exchanged knowing glances.

Tom scoffed. "Fine, Gene," he said. "Is there anything we can talk about?"

"Lots of things," Gene said. "But not that."

Tom looked away. He knew he'd gotten out of hand last summer with his Clinton-bashing rants, and Gene had every right to head off a repeat performance.

"You can talk about your turkeys, Tom," Gene said, and

the way he said *turkeys* made everybody laugh. Tom smiled despite himself. He did enjoy talking about the turkeys he raised and all the fits they gave him, and we never tired of hearing that.

Gene had revived the crew after an unsound start, but Rip had his own unfinished business to take care of. "How about O.J., Gene?" he said. "Can we talk about O.J.?" He laughed as Loni glared at him.

Gene drew in a deep breath. "Yeah, I suppose you can talk about O.J.," he said finally, with a pick-your-battles sigh. Rip cheered, and then Gene pulled out his clipboard and gave us our first painting assignments of the summer.

..

The project we were to tackle that summer was Aber Hall, the second of two eleven-story dorms on campus. Just as we'd done in eleven-story Jesse Hall five years before, during my first summer, we started at the top and completed three floors at a time. This system allowed us to make progress with minimal up-and-down travel.

Our first task on our first day—as it was every summer—was to rid all the rooms of the stench of Whatever Painters Came Before by cleaning off the old paint anywhere it wasn't supposed to be, such as on the wooden trim and cabinets, the rubber mopboard at the base of the walls, and the metal hinges and knobs on every door. This was standard procedure on any Gene job, and if we didn't do it right we did it again. He didn't give us any solvents or strippers—just told us to use paint scrapers and putty knives and to scrape as hard as needed to remove the long-dried errant paint. The process marred the wood, scratched the hinges, and took an inordinate amount of time, but Gene didn't give a shit as long as he didn't see old paint.

The next step in Gene's routine was to have us "gouge" all the holes in the plaster walls. It wasn't enough to just quickly fill the holes with spackle as normal painters might, especially in a dorm room; instead, we had to angle the edges of each hole at 45 degrees so that the spackle would disappear better into the smooth-wall finish. Even the tiniest pinholes needed to be gouged perfectly, or we would have to gouge again.

After gouging we filled the holes with heavy wet spackle that painters refer to as "mud." We did two coats of mud because it shrank; then we sanded vigorously because the dried mud was very solid. Gene always made us redo our sanding when we were done, or, as he put it, "start at the beginning and check everything over." Our groans and sighs did nothing to deter him.

After sanding we were ready to use tape and paper to "mask off" any unpainted surfaces. But in order to make the masking tape stick, we first had to make sure all the surfaces were free of dust and dirt. For this task, two crew members would strap on portable "back-vacs" and go from room to room vacuuming everything with a brush attachment. This was a fun job compared to most of what we did, and Gene usually reserved it for Rip and me, partly because he liked us and partly because the previous summer we'd invented a satirical TV show called *DormWatch*, which we acted out only when we had the back-vacs on.

In our show, Rip played the hero, Rygar, a lifeguard who lived in the dorms. In the first episode, "Bustin' Dust," the back-vac became a futuristic tool Rygar used to suck drowning people out of the ocean and to blast crooks with a fatal shot of fire. Rip, a David Hasselhoff look-alike with a chiseled athlete's body, played the role with surprising panache. He proved to be an incurable ham, exercising genuine improv skills, and I was his muse off to the side, a stock character when one was required. Transforming the tedium of dorm painting into an adventure-filled drama had enraptured the crew, inspiring Rip and me to create a new episode every time we got a chance to use the back-vacs. We would act out the scene while working, then relive it in the breakroom later. The crew laughed, and *DormWatch* was a hit.

But that was the previous summer. This summer had a darker edge to it, what with the televised O.J. trial and Gene's escalating battle with the union, and laughs among the crew were proving harder to come by. As Rip and I strapped on the back-vacs for the first time to do the top three floors of Aber Hall, I wondered if we'd write more episodes of *DormWatch* or if the series had perhaps jumped the shark.

..

It didn't take long for Rip to let me know we'd been picked up for another season. However, after performing an un-

inspired sequel to "Bustin' Dust"—the back-vac was now a
jet-pack piloted by Rygar, who flew up and down the dorm
halls rescuing coeds from intruding rapists—Rip turned off
his vacuum and attempted once again to draw me into his
ongoing spat with Loni over the O.J. mess. He tried to corner
me into agreeing out loud that Loni was old and naive. He
rehashed the debates they'd had over the first two weeks,
including a recent heated one about the "bloody glove" found
at the crime scene, the killer's bloody glove that spawned
lawyer Johnnie Cochran's infamous line to the jury: "If it
doesn't fit, you must acquit." Loni thought the sight of O.J.
pretending to try on the glove for the jury was the most
laughable bunch of bullshit she'd ever seen. Rip said it was
further reason to withhold judgment because, the fact was,
it didn't fit. Loni countered that the only "facts" she needed
were those pictures of Nicole's battered face.

Loni was so seriously pissed by then that Rip actually
shut up. Loni's propensity to detonate was renowned among
the crew. Once, when I was driving behind her on the way
out of the dorm parking lot at the end of the day, I'd seen her
get out of her car and scream like holy hell at another driver
who'd tried to pull in front of her. She just walked right up
to his window and let him have it face to face, with a fero-
cious, full-volume delivery that frightened the bejesus out
of me as I watched from the safety of my own driver's seat.
The woman had no fear.

"She has no clue how the system works," Rip said to me
now. "She's so fucking stupid."

"Mmmmm."

"She won't admit that I know just a little bit more about the law than she does."

"Uh-huh."

He seemed perturbed I wouldn't chime in, but Loni and I had developed a friendship over our five years together on the dorm crew. During the off-season Loni painted full time, and more than once she'd asked me to join her on a job, not as an employee but just to split the check. She generously shared the bounty from her garden, and sometimes when I stopped by to pick up a bag of vegetables she tossed in a couple of joints for good measure. During these visits we'd sit in her living room and talk. A few weeks ago when I'd been over, Loni had shown me her new computer smartly arranged on a desk in the corner of the living room. "I decided to buy myself a present," she said. "I'm going to get serious about writing again. I'm going to dig out my old manuscript and finish it." She'd smiled and looked away, thinking about the secrets that manuscript held, the possibilities. Her voice clicked with an unmistakable cadence of revived hope.

"Dude, she's a loser," Rip said now. "She's got a master's degree and she's a painter. If she thinks she's so much smarter than me, then why didn't she do something with her life?"

He gauged my silent reaction and soon realized he might have struck a glancing blow. "How old are you?" he asked as we got on the elevator down to tenth, and I sensed he was trying to reel it back a bit.

"Thirty."

"Really?" He thought about it. "I'm twenty-seven."

Twenty-seven and almost done with law school. Thirty and never finished college, a painter going on ten years in the trade. Rip was trying to figure out if I was a loser like Loni.

"Didn't you tell me once you were writing a novel?" he asked.

I was surprised he remembered, but not unhappy. "Uh-huh."

"What's it about?"

"I can't tell you that. Brings bad luck."

"Oh. Okay, whatever." He laughed. "Well, I want to read it when you're done. I can just imagine all the fucked-up shit that will come out of your head."

It was meant as a compliment, and I laughed too. "Actually, I will tell you what it's about—it's about you. I'm writing a book about what a jerk you are."

"Do it and I'll sue your ass," he said, and we both laughed again because he sounded serious.

..

"Where are you guys with the patch priming?" Gene asked. He was sitting at the head of the breakroom table.

"Middle of ninth," Loni said.

"Already?" He frowned. "You're being surgical, right?"

She sighed. "Yes, Gene, we're being surgical."

Most painters prime patches of spackle with a quick swipe of the brush; Gene demanded that we use small trim brushes and confine the primer strictly to the patch to prevent any excess "flashing," shiny spots in the topcoat that result from having primer underneath. Flashing is easy to overlook if you're so inclined, but Gene was not.

"Maybe I'll come up and take a look," he said.

"Oh Gene, give it a rest," Loni barked. "I just told you we're being surgical."

"Don't take it personally, Loni," Gene barked back, but he did seem to shelve the idea of an inspection, and Loni let it go. She'd been working under Gene for seven years. They might not be crazy in love, but as a pair of fifty-year-old painters, they at least knew enough to go easy on each other.

Gene dismissed us to our tasks but held me back. "You come with me. I've got a special job for you."

He took me to the tenth-floor bathroom and led me to the shower stalls. "You see that big crack up there? Where the walls meet the ceiling?" I nodded. The tiles had separated in an ugly, uneven manner that was only getting worse. Every shower stall was in the same shape.

"I've been wondering for weeks what to do about this," Gene said. "It's been keeping me awake at night."

I smiled only a little. He wasn't joking.

"I was going to use grout, but I decided to use caulk because I think it will stay flexible." He looked me in the eye. "What do you think?"

"Caulk makes sense to me."

"But can you make it look good?"

"Sure." Caulk is difficult to use on large cracks unless you know a few tricks; most people just smear it around and it looks like crap.

"I want it to look perfect. I don't want to hear from the squeezers that we screwed up the showers." The "squeezers" were the mop-squeezing custodial staff who worked in the building with us. By Gene's estimation they ranked even lower than painters, and he wanted to make sure it stayed that way.

I didn't disappoint Gene with the caulk, and the next day he made a special announcement in the breakroom. "If you get a chance, go check out the shower stalls on tenth. The caulk job is truly a work of art." He looked at me. "Thanks," he said, and I felt myself blush. When Gene said thanks about painting, he meant it.

··

As the summer advanced, the painters' union began sending out even more propaganda, bombarding us weekly through the mail. The August vote was quickly approaching, and the letters—always unsigned—were punctuated with desperate vitriol. The union outright accused Gene of telling lies about past incidents. They questioned his motives. They made unveiled attempts to scare us into voting union. One of the letters had a cartoon in which a patient lay strapped to a table while an evil doctor pushed a gas mask over the guy's mouth. The doctor was labeled "Idea Knocker," and he held a huge syringe labeled "Loyalty Oil." Another doctor standing next to him clutched a giant knife labeled "Fear." Off to the side a caption read: "A Most Delicate Operation . . . ," and above that a bottle of "Plasma Poison" floated in midair.

"Jesus, did you see that thing?" Loni asked me the day after it arrived. "I kept staring at it but could not figure out what the hell was going on."

"It was pretty bizarre."

"Idiotic is more like it." Loni never hesitated to inform somebody's word choice. She and I and a guy named Dexter were working in the hallway on sixth, painting metal door casings with dark blue, oil-based enamel. We had to cut the blue paint against the cream-colored walls, and it required close attention to make the line Gene-proof. Anything short of perfectly straight would be frowned upon.

Loni changed the subject. "I heard somebody say you were writing a novel."

I nodded.

"What's it about?"

"Just some stuff."

Her word-choice alarm buzzed again. "I assume it's about 'some stuff.' You don't want to tell me what kind of stuff?"

"I don't really like to talk about it."

"Oh, okay. Just say that then." She didn't sound upset.

"You're writing a novel?" Dexter said. He stopped painting and stared at me. "I've always had a lot of admiration for people who write novels. I could never do that." He lifted his eyes as if contemplating an enormous blank page. Dexter was a Vietnam veteran who now worked as a stone mason and painter. His face bore the deep lines of a hard life, but his eyes shone brightly above those dark canyons. Occasionally, he joined Loni and me on a side job during the off-season. He was a good painter and even better company.

"When are you going to finish it?" he asked.

"I'm almost done."

"Really?" Loni said. She stopped painting—a rarity. "I'm impressed. Most people never finish their so-called novels. They do most of their writing by talking about it in the bars." We all laughed. I wondered if she had done any work on her own manuscript, but I didn't ask and she didn't offer.

Dexter asked if I'd ever had anything published. I told him the big news from my life lately—that I'd just learned I was going to have a short story published in a magazine. "But," I added, "it's just a rock-climbing magazine. The story is about rock climbing."

"Hey," Loni said, "a published story is a published story. Congratulations."

"Yeah, congratulations," Dexter said. "You gotta start somewhere. Do they pay you for that?"

"About a thousand dollars."

"A thousand bucks?" Dexter said. "Holy crap, that's pretty good."

"Hell, yeah, it is," Loni said. Both she and Dexter congratulated me again. I marveled that they'd made me out to be exactly what I dreamed of being: an up-and-coming writer. For one moment I actually tasted what it could be like.

Then the elevator door at the end of the hall slid open with a *ding,* and a rambunctious group led by Billy Ames, son of the union boss, piled out. In the back of the pack I saw

Rip. As the gang headed our way, the three of us sighed and stiffened. Our comfortable conversation was over.

..

The temperature in the hall cooled considerably as Billy and his group got situated near us. They were performing a task Gene referred to as "crawling," in which we had to lie prone on the floor to look up at a narrow strip of wall hidden below the protruding, painted cinder block. This hidden half-inch strip would be ignored by most painters because the only way to see it was to lie flat on the floor. Gene couldn't care less about most painters, so we crawled.

Crawling all day was hard on a person's body and didn't require a whole lot of brains, so Gene usually assigned the task to crew members who either lacked good brushing skills or had some other quality that annoyed him. Billy Ames, for example, never escaped a crawl session, but I was surprised to see Rip crawling. Gene adored Rip.

"I can't believe Gene's making you crawl," I said when he got near.

"He's not making me. He asked me if I wanted to."

"Crawling sucks."

"No way, it's easy. You get to lie down all day."

"Yeah, lie down and *crawl*."

Loni and Dexter laughed. Billy Ames and the other two crawlers continued grunting along at a pace of about three feet a minute.

"Don't make fun of crawlers," Rip said. "It hurts our feelings."

"Oh, sorry. I didn't realize you crawlers were so sensitive."

"We are. We're very sensitive." Rip was sitting up now, ready to expound on crawlers. "And if you make us mad, we'll get you."

"Ooooh, we're scared," Loni said, but she laughed. Her smile showed she didn't want to be at war with Rip over O.J. all the time, but would rather be part of the fun too.

"You see, crawlers are an amazing breed," Rip said. "We look harmless lying on the floor. But when called to action, we respond like this!" He flew up into a full-alert crouch so quickly I jumped back. The move showcased his grace and athleticism, his tightened muscles beneath a short-sleeved shirt. Then he relaxed. "So you better watch out."

"No doubt," I said. "You crawlers are bad-asses."

"And don't you forget it." He lay back down on the floor and started crawling again.

"Do crawlers make a sound?"

"Yes, we do," Rip said. After a moment's pause, he came out with a weak chirp.

"That's it?" We laughed, thinking his improv skills had failed him this time, but he kept chirping. He added some awkward arm movements and head twists that made us laugh even more. Then Billy Ames and the other two started chirping and wiggling around, and before you knew it we had a whole herd of crawlers underfoot.

"Man, our brains must be seriously starved," Loni said when the chaos finally subsided. Rip opened his mouth to make a starved-brain crack about Loni, but then decided to let it go. The camaraderie in the hallway was that good. Right then there were no winners at life, no losers, no upwardly mobile students or stuck-in-place painters. Just a random group of people making the best of a shared moment.

It was nice, but it didn't last.

..

When Billy Ames crawled near me, he said, "Hey, nice conversation last night. You still coming to the union meeting tomorrow?"

Loni stopped painting in mid-stroke. I sent Billy a hush-hush look—I didn't spend an hour on the phone with you last night so you could toss me in the ring with Loni today—but he knew exactly what he was doing. Divide and conquer, that most classic battle strategy.

The phone call had been a surprise, though I probably should have expected it. Billy's voice had quavered as he identified himself and asked how I felt about the union situation. He reiterated the benefits of membership: retirement plans, insurance deals, loan programs, legal representation in a grievance. And the wage, of course—did I really think I was going to make $16.25 an hour on the outside? Come on, man, get real. This is a great deal and you know it—not to mention the unemployment we collect during the off-season. If it ain't broke, don't fix it. Right?

The money was the only issue I cared about. That wage financed my skiing and climbing the rest of the year, and I'd grown accustomed to the lifestyle. But even more than that, I was struck by the guts Billy displayed by calling. He knew I was tight with Gene, had even referred to me once as "Gene's pet," but he gave it a shot for his family's sake. He did it despite the fact that he did not have a strong personality—not like his dad, Vince, the union boss.

I'd met Vincent Ames one time when he'd come over from Great Falls for something other than our biennual contract renewal. He'd come to facilitate a training session about abating lead paint, a situation we often encountered at the university. He was an almost cardboard-cutout union man: big, loud, and curt in a way that strong-armed disagreement to the side. He managed this despite being afflicted with a stutter that completely contradicted his demeanor. He charged right over the pest and kept on going.

During the training session I had noticed how Billy orbited like a satellite off to the side of his father, smaller in stature but shining with accord. Billy didn't stutter, but he did shake a fair amount, his arms especially, an unfortunate encumbrance in a job that calls for steady hands. Once or twice during the abatement demonstration, Vince clipped out an order and Billy quickly complied in his jerky fashion, fighting to overcome the shake and perform for his father. Whatever hard-handed treatment had produced such trembling obedience had long ago been supplanted by loyalty and devotion.

The skills we learned in that workshop increased our value as professionals, and I'd come away with a better understanding not only of the Ames family but of the union's function too. Perhaps that's why I'd agreed over the phone to attend the emergency meeting tomorrow, even though I'd planned to skip it. "Just come hear what my dad has to say," Billy said, and I thought, why not? I don't hate the union. Sometimes I had a hard time understanding why anybody would.

..

Loni, on the other hand, had a hard time understanding why anybody wouldn't. She could give all kinds of reasons for her dislike, but I suspect more than anything it was her aversion to being controlled even slightly. When Billy started crawling away after having confirmed my commitment, she spoke for everybody in the hall to hear.

"By the way, Billy, I'd like to compliment you and your family on the cartoons you've been sending us in the mail. It's really intelligent stuff."

Billy looked at me and rolled his eyes.

"I guess you're not kidding when you say you're the first person in your family to go to college."

Billy stood. "Shut up, Loni."

"No, you shut up," Loni said, her rage uncoiling like a striking snake. "Your family has been living off us for years. Taking our money and not doing a damn thing for us. If you ask me, you're a bunch of crooks."

Billy moved toward her, his brush raised but his arms starting to quiver. "You don't know what the fuck you're talking about."

"Oh, yeah? Why did you shut down our local? Why did you take our car?" Loni was repeating two of Gene's primary gripes—how Vincent Ames had come to town one day nine years ago and shut down our local office, fired our business manager, and driven "our" car back to Great Falls. The car was a cheap Dodge Colt rarely used for union business, but the Missoula painters had it and then it was gone.

"It wasn't *your* car," Billy said, voice quavering with anger. "It belonged to the union."

"Well, why did you shut down our office?"

"Because there aren't enough union painters in Missoula to support an office."

"'There are more union painters in Missoula than in Great Falls!"

"But Great Falls is where the regional headquarters is," Billy hammered back, his entire body shuddering now. "Get it?"

"You mean Great Falls is where your *family* is. Get it?"

Billy turned and muttered, "Fuck you."

"Yeah, well, fuck you too. Shaky."

The cruel moniker smothered Billy into silence. Even Rip looked taken aback at Loni's viciousness. Then a loud *ding* issued from down the hall, and the elevator doors slid open. Gene emerged, pushing his bike. "Okay, you guys, square off!" he yelled.

··

"Square off" was perhaps Gene's favorite refrain. He liked to lower the tone of his voice about thirty degrees between the words, creating a trademark inflection. The literal meaning was to complete whatever you were painting to a "square" point, a natural edge or joint or corner, then stop and secure your tools. Gene hadn't invented the expression, but nobody in the world said it like he did.

"You guys heard him," Rip said. "Square off." He mimicked Gene's precise tone, and the joke seemed to douse the fire in the hall just enough. We suppressed our grins as Gene rolled up on his bike and stopped to inspect our doorjambs.

"Somebody's got a *sag*." He could have just described the most vile organism on earth.

"That's mine," Dexter said. "Sorry." He feathered out the run and then put his brush back in the paint bucket, stored the way Gene liked it: resting in two inches of paint with a rag covering the top of the can.

"Hey, Gene, I meant to ask you," Rip said. "How are your ears doing these days?"

Gene gave him a measured stare from between his red earmuffs. "Just fine, Rip. Thanks for asking."

"Sure." Rip smiled easily at the rest of us. Nobody else could get away with teasing Gene like that, but Rip had that certain power, like the most popular kid in the class. Not the nicest kid, but the one everybody curried for favor nonetheless.

Gene, for his part, seemed to enjoy tweaking people's perception of him. He wore the earmuffs to prevent a recurring ear infection he attributed to dust; he wore bright red earmuffs solely to confound observers. The bike was an eccentricity meant to save his failing feet—he had to travel miles up and down dorm hallways every day—but the whole getup taken together baffled other tradespeople on campus when they came into our dorm to work. "What's the deal with that guy?" I'd been asked more than once after Gene pedaled away. I liked to respond with a look that asked, what could you possibly be referring to?

..

The morning after the emergency union meeting, everybody was talking about it in the breakroom. This happened despite Gene's previous orders to avoid the topic, but he let it continue for a few minutes, probably because he was intensely curious not so much about the meeting but about the overall sentiment of the crew. He knew the career painters shared his views, but the college students were wild cards. Several of them hung out with Billy Ames and would likely vote union for their buddy. I saw Gene wrinkle his lips and silently assess the remaining temporary painters, the rookies and didn't-cares who would be deciding his fate.

"Hey, Gene, you should have heard what they said about you at that meeting," Loni said. She'd shown up at the union hall after happy hour and been a vocal critic.

"Me?" Gene frowned. "What did they say about me?"

"That you're a liar."

"Nobody said that, Gene," Billy Ames cut in.

"Yes, they did, Billy," Loni said. "That's exactly what they said." Bottled fuel from their argument in the hall the other day had been building pressure inside her. You could tell by the way she talked that it was only a matter of seconds until it foamed out of her mouth.

"Okay, you guys, that's enough union talk," Gene said.

"Nobody called you a liar at the meeting, Gene," Billy repeated.

"I don't care what they said about me, Bill, to be honest."

"Well, I just want you to know—"

Loni jumped in. "Why should we believe you or your family about anything? All you've done is lie to us over the years."

Billy's chair zoomed backward, banging into a bookshelf. "We're *not* liars, you bitch. You don't know the first thing about my family. You—"

Loni's chair tipped over as she jumped up, a furious babble of words starting to tumble forth.

"Okay, you guys, enough!" Gene barked, slamming his book down on the table. Gene always kept a novel in the breakroom and spent most of his spare time reading it, largely to avoid getting ensnared in our often inane conversations. That summer he was rereading *Catcher in the Rye*. He'd told me he wanted to have a little "fun."

Both Loni and Billy sat back down. They were angry, but neither wanted to exchange blows with the opposite sex at seven-thirty in the morning.

Gene cleared his throat. "Okay, then." He turned to me. "So. Where are you rollerheads?"

"Fourth."

"How about you brush-heads?"

"Fifth," Loni muttered.

"Okay. Everybody just pick up where you left off." He stood to dismiss us.

"Hey, Gene, what about Garbology?" Rip asked before anybody moved. "Yeah, yeah, what about Garbology?" somebody else said. "Yeah? Yeah?"

Gene sighed and sat back down. As much as he wanted to disperse the crowd, nothing eclipsed the importance of Garbology.

"All right, let's do it quick. Whose turn is it to ask the question?"

I raised my hand because I'd lost the previous week. The punishment was to empty the breakroom garbage cans in the dumpster behind the dorm, but the hidden reward was that you got to ask the question the next week.

"Okay, what's the question?"

I was ready. "The question is . . ." Everybody waited. "What's the balance of my checking account?" I held up my checkbook. The usual grumbling began.

"That's the stupidest question I've ever heard."

"What kind of a question is that?"

"This is lame, Gene. Make him ask another question."

"That question is kind of a dog," Gene muttered, even as he wrote a number on a scrap of paper. *Dog* was the name he usually reserved for old paint brushes that had developed hopelessly errant bristles—Gene castrated their handles and turned them into dusters.

But the question stood, and people began eyeing me intensely, trying to see into aspects of my character they'd never given much thought to. It was exactly the puzzlement you look for in a Garbology question, and I smiled as I held out a painter's cap and fielded scraps of paper. When everybody was in, I sat down.

"So what's the answer?"

"Negative forty-seven dollars. Good thing tomorrow is payday."

Groans and hoots erupted all around. "I said zero!" Rip shouted. "I'm safe." Gene looked a little worried as I opened the answers, but Loni ended up losing by a large margin. Loni actually had terrible luck at Garbology. You'd think the game would be similar to crossword puzzles, but it wasn't, and losing bruised her desire to be taken seriously as an intellectual.

"Sorry about that," I said as she grabbed the garbage cans and grunted toward the door.

"I guess I had a little too much faith in you," she said. "Thought you planned a little better than that."

"Yeah, well." I followed her down the hall and opened the outside door, then lifted the heavy dumpster lid while she unloaded the cans.

"Thanks," she said sincerely. Loni's fifty-year-old body ached of painting, I saw it every day. Not that I ever heard her complain.

"No problem," I said, holding the door again as we walked back into the dorm. "Hey . . . do you mind if I stop by sometime?"

She rolled her eyes slightly. So that's what was behind the opened doors: "vegetables."

"Sure."

"Cool. When?"

"Oh, any time," she said in mock whimsy, turning her back to me. "I don't have a life, don't you know that by now?"

··

My duty for the day was rolling ceilings, so after leaving Loni I hustled up the stairwell to the fourth floor, where I'd left off the day before. Walking down the hall, I heard Gene's voice and wondered why. He usually had more important things to do than get me going.

"There you are," he said when I walked into the room. Billy Ames stood in front of him, Rip off to the side. "I've decided you guys need some help," Gene said, handing me my roller pole. "I want you to show Billy how to roll a ceiling."

I hesitated. Gene was a ceiling freak. The first thing he did when he walked into any room was look at the ceiling and frown as he scoured the surface for roller lines, excessive stipple, missed spots (known as "holidays"), or protruding stalactites of grit and glop. In the dorms, much to Gene's displeasure, all the walls were smooth plaster, having been built before the textural rages of the 1970s. The paint job was the texture, there was no faking it, and after a disgusted sigh Gene would shake his head and lower his eyes.

Rip was my usual partner when rolling ceilings. I'd trained him to do it the way Gene had trained me. Rip excelled at rolling ceilings, maybe because he knew ceilings were a top priority for Gene and he wanted to prove his worth, or maybe because working a roller pole above his head allowed him to showcase his arm muscles in the dormroom mirrors all day. Whatever his motivation, Rip was the only one besides me who Gene trusted to keep the dorm ceilings out of his nightmares. So what the heck was Billy Ames doing here?

"Ah, we're waiting," Gene said to me, and Rip laughed.

..

Exhaling, I tried to focus. Even after five years and countless affirmations, painting in front of Gene still made me nervous.

First I wet the roller in a five-gallon bucket filled halfway with paint, then evened out the load by running the nap on a metal ramp set inside the bucket. When the nap was wetted just so—good and soaked but not actively dripping—I raised the roller pole and began applying paint to the ceiling in long, sweeping strokes. I dipped frequently and spread the paint quickly and consistently. When I reached the end, I put the roller in the bucket and stood back.

"Great job," Billy Ames said, sounding bored.

"He's not done, Bill," Gene said as if speaking to the world's biggest dolt.

Billy nodded uncertainly, then stayed quiet while we waited. Rip stood with his arms folded, resenting Gene for making him sit through a refresher but knowing there was no help for it. Nobody said anything for six or seven minutes.

Finally, the timer rang in my head, a regulator refined over time that processed the room's air temperature, amount of circulation, and level of humidity, then combined that information with the relative thickness of the paint and the accepting (or not) nature of the surface to which it was applied. When all these factors coalesced, I knew the moment of lay-off had arrived.

..

When I finished laying off the ceiling, Gene walked around slowly and inspected it, not frowning, almost marveling. He'd seen how I'd divided the ceiling into a right half and a left half, laying off the roller strokes into the center by gently lifting and following through. He'd seen how I'd overlapped my strokes just the right amount, applying slightly less pressure to the "upstream" side to prevent leaving behind any discernible lines; how I got close to the walls without bumping, closer even to the light fixture in the center of the ceiling. More than anything, he'd heard the kind of stipple he adored—like Velcro being pulled apart. Time it just right and you get tight and tiny rather than sagging and smeared. Gene knew that the proper application of paint requires two steps: laying it on and laying it off. Bad painters just lay it on and leave it. Good painters understand the importance of laying it off.

"Did you see that, Bill?" he asked. Billy nodded. "Good. Now let's have you do one." He turned to Rip. "You can go."

Gene, Billy, and I moved to the next room. Billy commenced to shaking as he lifted the roller up to the ceiling, but he maintained a look of stubborn confidence.

"Ah, you're dripping," Gene said, pointing at the window where a splooge had landed. Startled, Billy set down the roller and wiped the window clean. Then he lifted the roller again and continued laying on paint, fighting a rising vibration in his nervous arms. When he got near a wall he bumped it, leaving behind a thick glob.

"No, Bill, that's exactly what we *don't* want," Gene said. This feared phrase was Gene's most disparaging assessment of painting incompetence, reserved for extreme situations, and again Billy stopped.

"I'll wipe it off when I'm done," he said finally and kept going, making sure to keep the roller far away from the walls.

"Christ, Bill, you've got to get closer than that," Gene said. "Just don't hit it. It's not that difficult."

"Gene, just let me do it . . ." Billy sputtered, but Gene continued to condemn every aspect of his work, including telling him at least three times to use more paint.

When Billy had finished laying on the ceiling, he was a sweaty mess. He set the roller in the bucket, wiped the wall where he'd hit it, and stood back to rest.

"I think you better start laying it off now, Bill. That took way too long."

Billy inhaled deeply. Grimly, he picked up the roller and started laying off the ceiling. But as much as he wanted to force smooth strokes on that surface, he failed to quell the curse that jostled him through life like an ever-present devil, bumping his elbow every time he tried to sign his name. Watching him battle that demon was enough to make a person want to leave the room. I had to stay.

"Ah, Bill, Bill," Gene kept saying, as if he'd given up trying to find words to describe such erratic blundering. Billy kept going but the paint was drying on him, setting up in an awfully uneven manner. The ceiling was about thirty seconds away from being totally beyond rescue.

"Nope, Bill, you're losing it," Gene said, and in one hard motion he knocked Billy to the side and confiscated the roller.

"Damn it, Gene, just let me finish," Billy said, but Gene showed no evidence of hearing as he set out to save the ceiling. He applied more paint as he went, laying it off immediately in short steps, a tactic he normally detested but was now required as an emergency measure. It took fifteen minutes of single-minded, hard-grunting effort, but in the end Gene succeeded.

Exhaling strongly, he set the roller in the bucket and turned to Billy.

"Okay, Bill, I think we have a change of plans here. I want you to go clean buckets in the sink room until I figure out something else for you to do." Cleaning buckets in the sink room occupied the lowest rung on our chore ladder.

"I know how to paint a ceiling, Gene, if you'd let me—"

"Just go, Bill," Gene snapped. Billy glared furiously and then stalked out, smacking the doorjamb with the butt of his hand as he passed.

Gene picked up his clipboard. "Well, that was a disaster," he said simply as he examined his papers. He showed no hint of being pleased that the son of the union boss couldn't paint a ceiling, and I can't say for certain that the episode was about anything other than Gene's quest for the perfect stipple. All I can say is that in five years, I never knew him to overlook irony.

..

A few days later I stopped by Loni's house. I had no idea where she scored weed, but she was well connected to the graying hippie/artist contingent in Missoula, so it didn't seem strange.

She lived alone in a small Craftsman on the north side of town. Often she was sitting on the front porch when I came over, sipping a drink and reading, but today the porch was empty. I walked through the gate and around to the backyard, figuring to find her crouched in the garden. The garden was empty but the back door to her house was cracked open, so I leaned inside and shouted a greeting. Nothing. I pushed the door all the way open and stepped into the kitchen.

"Loni?"

I heard a muffled reply that seemed to come from under the house, and then I noticed stairs in the corner of the kitchen that led down to a basement. Loni's voice came from down there. I hesitated, not wanting to barge in on something I shouldn't see, but a moment later she elbowed through the door and emerged carrying an armload of soaking wet paper.

"My basement flooded," she said grimly. "I haven't even been down there since that last rain. Look at this." She held up the paper. "My manuscript. It's ruined." She tossed the heavy pile of pages onto the kitchen table. The ink had run to oblivion or simply disappeared on the parts I could see.

Loni, too, stared at the pile. "It's my own stupid fault. I had everything stored up on shelves, but I pulled this out a few months ago to look at it. Just left it there like an idiot. Years of work." She muttered her dismayed epitaph over the papers. "And I don't have another copy. It was all written on a typewriter."

I shook my head and uttered condolences.

Just like that her toughness kicked in. "Oh well, fuck it," she said. "Come on." She waved me into the living room and we sat down. "So. What's going on?"

"Not much. How about you?"

"Oh, nothing much." She reached over and picked up her drink. If she was an alcoholic, she was a fully functional one.

"That's too bad about your manuscript. Maybe you can salvage some of it."

She nodded and looked out the window. "I wonder what my mother would say," she mused, the query thick with sarcasm. "I know what she'd say. She'd call me stupid for leaving it on the basement floor, and she'd be right. Then she'd tell me for the thousandth time I should have gone to law school." She lit a cigarette. "And you know what? She's right about that too. I should have gone to law school, then I wouldn't be painting dorms right now. But noooo, I had to be a writer." She shook her head in wonder. I glanced over at the computer she'd shown me a few months ago, her "present to herself." Clothes hung on the chair, and the once-clear desk was cluttered with random items.

"What is your mother like?" she asked.

"My mother?" This whole mother conversation had

caught me by surprise. "She's fine." I gave it a bit more thought. "I guess she's not too thrilled about the fact that I'm a painter."

The life ring was right on target and Loni grabbed it. "God, isn't it the truth? Sometimes I think it's the only thing my mother thinks about, even after all these years. She never wants to talk about all the beautiful things I'm growing in my garden, or books or movies or anything like that. All she wants to do is criticize my life and remind me that I never had kids." Her face hardened again. "I guess that's why I never talk to her anymore."

I nodded, hoping she wouldn't ask me if I still talked to my mother. I loved my mother.

"So, how's your novel coming?" she asked with distraction.

"Good," I said before I could stop myself. Hers was ruined.

But she didn't take it poorly. "Good," she said. She looked at me, her eyes softening. "Where do you live these days?"

I told her.

"Still renting?"

"Yep."

"You should think about buying," she said. "Seriously."

I nodded politely. The last thing I wanted was heavy mortgage payments tugging at my freedom to ski and climb. Of course, I didn't know Missoula was set to explode over the next ten years as a hip Rocky Mountain destination city; to me it was just the same old lazy college town it had always been. So I ignored—no, hardly even heard—the best financial advice anybody ever gave me, before or since.

Loni gauged my distaste and retreated immediately, memories of her mother's haranguing beating her back. In short order she went to the kitchen and returned with a brown paper sack, which she handed to me. It was heavy with tomatoes and peppers and whatever else. I didn't look, because I knew Loni. A few minutes later I said goodbye and left her alone.

..

ONE MAN DOESN'T MAKE A PARADE!

To: All University Painters

From: International Brotherhood of Painters and Allied Trades (IBPAT)

When a parade comes down the street, it is the leader out front who first catches everyone's attention. Whether it is a tall band leader in a glittering uniform, a top-hatted big shot, or a pretty baton-twirling majorette, it is the leader who gets first attention. Often people are so impressed or mad at the leader that they don't remember the rest of the parade. They get to thinking that the leader is the whole show.

That's what certain individuals in Missoula would like to have you think about General Representative Vincent Ames. They'd like you to forget the people, just like yourself, who make up Local Union 260. They would have you believe that Local Union 260 is simply there to benefit a few leaders. They think if they can get all of your attention focused on the leader you'll forget the rest of the parade.

Leaders are important in Unions but—just like a parade—they are not the whole show by any means. **IT IS YOU THE MEMBERS**, all working together for the common welfare, that makes Local 260 a great parade. Anybody who says you can get more and have more by throwing the Union out is living in a never never land. Just ask Brother Hank Carroll. He worked for the county maintenance department when they decertified. Over a period of time they started to lose wages, benefits, and working conditions. It got so bad Hank quit and came to work at the University. **ASK BROTHER HANK CARROLL WHAT HE THINKS ABOUT THE UNION!**

Don't sit on the sidelines and let the parade pass by you. Voice your disapproval to those individuals who would take away a better life for you and your family. **REMEMBER, YOU ARE THE 'U' IN UNION.**

..

"I want you to help me write a response," Gene said.

"Me?"

"Yeah. You're a writer, aren't you?"

"I guess so."

He smiled wryly into the windshield of the work van. We were on our way to the paint store. Gene often brought me on his errands to keep him company, probably because as a general rule I only spoke when he spoke to me, unless I really had something that would make him laugh. We spent a lot of time riding in a comfortable silence that seemed to encourage Gene to take the long way around, which was fine by me.

"I thought you were writing a novel," he said.

"I am." He must have heard somebody else talking about it, because I'd never discussed it with him.

"Well, don't worry, I won't ask you what it's about."

"Everybody else does."

"'A boy and his dog,'" Gene said, "that's all you have to say. It's about a boy and his dog."

I laughed. "Sounds good to me."

"Yeah." When I didn't inquire about the source of this insider tip, Gene provided an explanation. "I wrote a novel once."

"Really?"

He nodded. "Right when I got out of the Navy. I had some extra time so I just sat down and wrote it."

"Huh." I sensed a foreign note of fragility in his voice. "So what happened?"

"Well, I gave it to everybody in my family to read."

"That took guts."

He didn't respond.

"So did they like it?"

"No, they hated it," he said. "They laughed at me and said, 'Who are you to think you can write a novel? Who are you?'"

"You're kidding. They said that to you?"

"Yes."

"That's pretty lame."

He didn't reply.

"So what did you do?"

"What did I do?" He looked out the window, his voice hazy with rekindled embarrassment. "I put the novel in the bottom of my seabag, that's what I did. Underneath all my old Navy crap."

"Oh."

"And as far as I know it's still there, although I can't say for certain because I never looked at it again."

I opened my mouth, wanting to say something—wanting to show Gene the respect he'd been robbed of all those years ago, to tell him that even though he was a painter he was smart enough to write a novel worth reading. But I knew he'd revisited that hurtful episode enough for one day, so I said nothing. After a minute he steered the conversation back toward the letter he wanted me to help him write. He had a lot of points he wanted to make. Would I come over to his house after work and help him? Of course I said yes. It's not like I didn't owe him.

..

That evening I went over to his house. To my relief, Gene had already written a rough draft longhand. Mostly he wanted help using his new computer, a model similar to Loni's with a floppy drive. Once I got him going on that, he pecked slowly at the keyboard until I offered to take over— the hand-written letter was four pages long. Gene agreed, stood up, and started to dictate.

I focused on sentence structure and punctuation. Several times he asked me what I thought of the letter, if it was good. I said yes, it's good, and I wasn't lying. But I also wasn't contributing any passion to the process, and we both knew it. As I typed I felt Gene's attention on me, wondering how I would vote, hoping to hear just one word against the union come out of my mouth.

He didn't hear it. He got his answer.

··

"How are you going to vote, man?"

"None of your business."

"Come on," Rip said. "If you tell me, I'll tell you."

We were rolling ceilings on the second floor, the crew having now descended to the final phase of the painting project, which encompassed the bottom three floors and the basement. It was Monday of our second-to-last week of work, and the union vote was scheduled for Thursday. Although there had been surprisingly little discussion of the union business throughout the summer, it seemed the entire crew had shown up this morning with an awakened interest, realizing the vote was actually going to happen. We stood around outside the building and in the hallways, speaking quietly and glancing around at the other small groups gathered. For this week at least, everybody seemed to have forgotten about O.J.

I surveyed Rip suspiciously. "Did Gene ask you to ask me?"

"Not exactly," he said. "But he did ask me to gauge the 'mood' of the temporary painters."

The pitch-perfect way Rip said *mood* brought a clear image of Gene into my head, and I felt a poke of jealousy. I should have been Gene's spy.

"So I take it you're voting to get out of the union?" I said.

"Sure," Rip replied. "Not because I really care, but just to support Gene."

I felt another poke. Shouldn't I be supporting Gene? "I don't think people should overlook what the union does for us. It might be one of those things you never really see until it's gone."

"Maybe," he said, "but come on. Do you really think it makes sense for the university to be paying temporary student painters $16.25 an hour?"

"We're not all students."

"You know what I mean."

"Not really. This is how I make my living."

"Dude, come on," he said. "Do you really think you're going to be painting dorms for the rest of your life?" He laughed in disbelief. I suppose I should have been flattered, especially with all my daydreaming about my novel and how I was going to establish literary stardom. But I was thirty years old and had been painting since I was nineteen, so it was untrue to say I wasn't invested.

"Maybe you shouldn't vote at all," I said. "Since you don't care."

"Yeah, I thought about that. But some day I might want to get into politics, and it looks bad to miss an election, any election." He smiled. "I've voted in every election I've ever been eligible for. School bonds, city council, you name it."

"You're kidding?" I believed him, though. Rip was meticulous about planning his future and intent on keeping his record clean. One day in the breakroom the crew got to talking about partying, and Rip announced that he'd never even held a cigarette between his lips—lit or unlit. *Never?* we said. Never, he said, and we all howled, but with Rip you knew it was true the same way you knew he'd show up at work every morning with his hair perfectly moussed while the rest of us straggled in like war refugees. Nothing was going to stop him from achieving success, not even unkempt hair among painters at seven-thirty in the morning.

"Anyway," he said, "I'm voting with Gene. He's the one who's going to be left behind after we leave, and if he wants out of the union then that's good enough for me."

The idea of Rip leaving the crew was a downer. We'd worked together three summers while he made his way through law school, but now our relationship would surely end. One of us had outgrown the other.

"Rip, why do you want to be a lawyer?" I asked.

"Why?" He sounded surprised, then shrugged. "Money."

"Money? That's it?"

"Pretty much. And it will be a challenge. I'll get to use my brain." He seemed to eye me as an example of a life spent otherwise, now that I'd admitted my allegiance to painting's monotonous grind.

"You'll be wasting your brain, if you ask me."

"Wasting my brain?" He laughed. "How so?"

"Don't you think you could do something a little more creative than being a lawyer? I mean, how boring is that?"

He laughed again. "Not nearly as boring as this. And it pays a hell of a lot better."

"Rip," I said, "this is going to sound strange, but I really think you could be an actor if you wanted to. You're a natural ad-libber, and to me your delivery seems perfect. And you've got the looks, and the build, and I know this sounds strange, but I seriously think you could get on television if you wanted to. I think you could do it."

He laughed. "You're not serious." Still, he couldn't help shooting a glance toward the dorm-room mirror. His chiseled chest and arms were perfect, but it was his face that set him apart. Finely formed bones accentuated intelligent eyes that invited all comers to join in on the joke, to ride along with Rip because he knew where he was going.

"I am serious," I said. "Why not just give it a shot? Why not go out to Hollywood and see what happens? Meet with an agent, see what they say. Hell, go straight to *BayWatch* and see if you can get on. If they see you, man, if they talk to you, I think you have a legitimate shot."

"You're fucking crazy."

Nonetheless, I watched his face soften as his mind switched from dismissing the impossible to imagining the possibilities. Was I nutty, or was there something to it? What if he went about it the same way he went about everything else, with meticulous planning and unshakable confidence? What if he plowed through Hollywood the same way he plowed through offensive linemen as a college football star, or through competitive classes at a top-notch law school, or through every other challenge he'd ever encountered? If he put everything he had into achieving the dream, what could possibly stop him?

"Nah," he said, and it was like he'd been invisible and had reappeared.

"Nah?"

"My old man would shit."

"Your old man? Who gives a fuck about your old man?"

He laughed, but then swallowed. "You don't know my old man."

I argued with him for a while, but it soon became apparent I had no chance against the old man. But as certain as Rip sounded about his future, he couldn't hide a hint of regret in his voice, as if he truly would enjoy a chance to succeed as an actor—but now he'd never get to try. A sprout of doubt had popped out where none existed before, as if somebody had planted it there on purpose to show him that painters aren't the only ones who get to question their life choices.

..

The day of the union vote I showed up at work early. Loni sat on a bench outside the dorm, smoking a cigarette. It was a nice day, and I sat down beside her. The sky was a bright dark blue; the campus was green and well kept. Some days I didn't enjoy the sense of demotion that came with being a painter on the campus where I used to be a student, but other days I found myself looking around and thinking what a beautiful place it was to work. I was lucky to be making

$16.25 an hour in Missoula, Montana, a tough place to eke out a living by any measure.

"So, did you hear about the union vote?" Loni asked. Then she fell into one of her deep, hard coughing fits. She didn't do this often, but when she did it was brutal to watch.

When she was done, I said, "What about it? It's today after work, right?"

She shook her head. "Nope. They cancelled it."

"Cancelled it? How could they cancel it?"

"Gene filed an emergency petition to postpone the vote, and apparently the union went along with it. They're going to wait until after we're gone." She sucked on her cigarette. "I heard about it late last night. Gene will probably make an announcement this morning."

"Wait until after we're gone? That means the temporaries won't be able to vote."

She nodded. When our work stints ended at the university, the union required us to file "withdrawal" cards, suspending our active status. They charged us $50 apiece to do it, but in exchange we were relieved from paying dues all winter. The caveat was that they gave exactly one chance to withdraw every fall, and if you missed it you needed to either pay dues all winter or quit outright and pay another $350 activation fee in the spring. None of the temporaries could afford to stay active all winter just to vote.

"Why do you think they did it?"

"Because we're too much of a wild card. There are fifty of us statewide, compared to the fourteen full-time guys. Nobody knew how we'd vote, so both sides decided not to take the chance. Apparently, both sides think the full-time guys will swing their way. Personally, I think a lot of them are talking out both sides of their mouth."

We sat in silence for a minute. Loni had a crossword puzzle folded on her lap, but it showed no sign of action. I glanced at her face; she seemed all-in, not anywhere near her normal snappiness.

"Everything all right?"

I hoped for a snarling defense but got only a quiet confession.

"Oh . . . not really, I guess." She cleared her throat. "I pulled a baddie last night."

"A baddie?"

"Yeah," she said, sounding mesmerized by a familiar predicament. "Getting drunk, calling customers." She shook her head. "I called the lady I've been doing that kitchen for. You know the side job I told you about?"

I nodded.

"Yeah, well . . . let's just say I don't know if I'm working there anymore." She tossed her cigarette on the grass and watched it burn.

I'd seen Loni snarl at customers a few times. Mostly they cowed, which diminished them in her view. She'd growled at me once when we were painting a house together, and the next day I presented her with a plan that divided the house in two halves—you do your half and I'll do my half. She apologized and I accepted, but I still made her split the job. She never growled at me again, preferring to keep me around to lift the heavy ladders and get the high hard spots.

Loni glanced at her watch and pulled out one last cigarette. "Well, what's done is done. I'll just have to go over there after work and apologize."

"I'm sure she'll understand."

She sighed at my silliness. "Maybe."

I got up and walked into the dorm, but the taint of Loni's depression stuck to my clothes and hair. Her sad, tired eyes could see nothing but a life that would only get harder as she entered her Golden Years—so different from the well-off women whose kitchens she painted. I wished I could help her lift all those heavy ladders ahead, but seeing her like that made me more certain than ever that I didn't want to end up like her. An old painter. A failed writer.

..

TO: ALL UNIVERSITY MAINTENANCE PAINTERS

You probably have already heard what the results of the decertification election were.

If you haven't, there were seven (7) votes for the International Brotherhood of Painters and Allied Trades and seven (7) votes for NO Representation at all. When a tie vote exists the Labor Department takes this to mean that no bargaining representation exists because the individuals voting didn't vote in a majority. In order for a Union to represent you, 50% of you plus (1) must vote for the Union.

The results of this vote also means that you are no longer represented by anyone at all. You are at the complete mercy of the employer (University System). The contract that you once enjoyed is no longer in effect. The employer has the right to set forth your wages, terms and conditions of employment. As an example, they could set forth a wage structure different than you are presently getting. They could raise or lower it at will. The employer will have this privilege for at least a year.

At the end of the year, another election could be held wherein you would have the choice of selecting a representative or continuing your NO representation status.

For the seven (7) individuals who voted to have the union represent you, we thank you from the bottom of our hearts. No doubt we have made some mistakes but they were honest mistakes.

Arrangements have been made for those of you that might want to continue your membership in the Painters Union elsewhere. For further details, call Vince Ames.

GOD BLESS YOU AND YOUR FAMILY. WE WISH YOU THE BEST FOR THE FUTURE!

..

Within six months of the decertification vote, the university cut the hourly wage of the temporary painters in half, from \$16.25 to \$8.50. Temporaries who had previously been working under the union contract were grandfathered in at a wage of $12.70 an hour, the same wage paid to the full-timers like Gene. Our $3.55-an-hour benefits compensation went the way of most blue-collar benefits these days—poof—and all newly hired painters would be working for a helper's wage.

I didn't return to the crew the following summer, and I never saw Gene or talked to him about what happened. Once he stopped by my house when I wasn't home. He left a large note on the windshield of my car telling me to call him if I was looking for work that summer. I guess he wanted me to know it was nothing personal, that he just needed the extra $100-a-month he used to pay in dues, and he had gambled correctly that the university would not mess with the full-timers' compensation, only the temporaries. He knew who would be left behind.

As for Loni, she never returned to the dorm crew either. Her life took a fresh twist when she met a guy and they started hanging out. He was about her age, maybe a few years younger, a scraggly misfit until you talked to him and realized he had it together. He worked as a wildlife biologist for the state, which is about as steady as it gets in Montana.

Eventually, Loni sold her house and bought one with her boyfriend, a bigger home with a shop out back that she could use as a base for her painting business, an enterprise she now had the luxury of operating at a more relaxed pace. The two of them also bought a small apartment building downtown and fixed it up; it was so successful they bought another. Loni would talk to me about these investments when I stopped by to pick up a bag of vegetables. I would sit in the living room with her and her boyfriend, admiring her renewed enthusiasm as she mixed another drink for the two of them, so much better than one at a time. I was apt to stay longer and talk longer because having a third person there made things more comfortable. Watching Loni defer to her boyfriend was strange, but she seemed content to be tamed.

Occasionally, Loni would ask me what my "plans" were, and I sensed she wanted things to work out for me, as they had for her. She was wary not to judge, though, and perhaps that's why she never asked me directly about what happened to my novel. She probably figured I never finished it after all.

Well, I did finish it. Then I gave it to a writing professor, a guy who'd encouraged me after reading some of my stories in a workshop and had agreed to help me with the manuscript. He wasn't a famous writer, but he had an agent and other connections to get it into the right hands.

The day I handed him the novel, he made the joke of dropping his arm like the load weighed fifty pounds. He asked me how long it was, and I said 750 pages. He smiled and said he'd call me.

Two weeks later he did call. "I'm not going to read your novel."

"You're . . . not?"

"No."

"Why not?"

"Because there's no tension."

"No tension?" My heart was pounding, my gut tightening.

"Yeah," he said. "I've read about 200 pages. But every

time I sit down to read it, I find myself looking for something else to do. So . . ."

So it sucks, I thought. Okay. We arranged for me to stop by his office that afternoon and pick it up. In his office we sat and discussed a few specifics, but it seemed like we were just going through the motions. I felt lightheaded, jarred by the blow. He truly thought the novel sucked. Worse, he sounded sincerely disappointed. I'd been so certain of my brilliance. Could I really have made such a grievous miscalculation?

I drove home and went straight into my bedroom. I pulled the manuscript out of the bag and set it on the bed. I winced at the decorated box I'd made for it, how I'd envisioned the cover of my book—it looked so amateurish now. Two years of scheming and dreaming reduced to complete naïveté. Who are you to think you can write a novel? Who are you?

Hot humiliation scorched my face as I searched the room for a dark hiding spot. In the closet I found an old chest of worthless crap, and in one sure motion I buried the novel deep inside and never looked at it again.

5

---

fathers and sons

Throughout my twenties and early thirties, I worked for about ten different painting companies in addition to my regular summer stints with the university's housing department. Some of these contractors allowed me to quit and come back multiple times. They might not have been thrilled that I was taking off on another climbing or skiing trip, but as long as I worked hard and gave ample notice, all I had to do when I ran out of money was pick up the phone and ask to be put back on—if they had work, the answer was yes; if not, I'd call somebody else.

Each crew was its own soap opera, and you never knew who you were going to end up with. I shared a motel room in Spokane once with a guy who'd done ten years for manslaughter. Our crew had traveled over from Montana to paint a new big-box store, and the boss set us up on a dingy street favored by prostitutes and crack dealers, amenities the rest of the crew didn't hesitate to indulge. When my roommate told me he had hepatitis so I shouldn't touch his razor in the bathroom, I recall really wanting to get out of Spokane.

The point is, I'm ordinary compared to most painters. My life is boring; theirs, full of adventure. Ironically, most painters I worked with didn't see it that way—they considered *me* crazy because of my rock-climbing compulsion. But as I watched them deal with their everyday disasters, I was always perplexed by how they managed to casually confront such severe challenges. From multiple addictions to multiple divorces, kids out of wedlock to more kids out of wedlock, probation violations and home evictions to just about every other personal problem you can think of, these guys kept chugging along as if their desperate straits were no big deal. Usually. Every so often a crew member succumbed to external pressures and disappeared, leaving the rest of us to wonder what happened. This is the story of one such exit.

··

Hank had a hole in his head. He talked about it as we set up scaffolding in the produce aisle of a supermarket on a Sunday evening.

"Happened down in Mississippi." His deep voice drew the attention of some nearby shoppers. Hank was a large man who seemed even more giantlike standing among the vegetables. "I was climbing a ladder one day, and another guy was above me. He was tailing his nail gun below him, and it bumped my head. Thap!" He mimed the way a touch-activated nail gun jumps in a carpenter's hand when fired. The listening shoppers gave a collective twinge.

"I even have a picture of it," he said, "an X-ray. Shows the nail sticking straight into my skull almost three inches. The doctor said a hair to the left or a hair to the right and I'd be dead." He smiled at his audience. "A hair, get it?" Again the laugh boomed.

"So now," he said, bending over to lift an aluminum plank above his shoulders and toss it onto the scaffold, where it rattled into place with a dusty shudder, sprinkling some nearby bananas, "I'm just waiting on my settlement." He pulled out a pack of cigarettes. "Those nail guns were defective. They had no safety catch on the trigger. Lots of lawsuits came out of it, and I'm in line for a couple hundred grand." He flicked a lighter and drew deeply, then blew the exhaust into the air.

The customers wrinkled their noses and looked annoyed. After appraising Hank's imposing frame, though, they kept quiet.

"Hank," I said, pointing at the cigarette.

"You should see the car I got picked out," he said. "I'll drive it to work one of these days. The dealer lets me take it out sometimes because he knows I'm going to buy it as soon as I get my money." He chuckled. "In fact, I'm not even supposed to be working now—it might screw up the lawsuit. We're saying I suffer from dizzy spells." He sniffed and took another puff of the cigarette. "Actually, I do suffer from dizzy spells sometimes."

"Excuse me." The supermarket's assistant manager had walked up and now stood in Hank's shadow. "You can't do that in here."

"Can't do what?" Hank looked around. "Oh, shit!" His deep laugh filled the grocery store. "I'm sorry—I totally forgot where we were. Sorry." He mashed the cigarette on his shoe, then put it in his pocket. "Sorry," he said again, but with a tone indicating the matter ends right here.

Hank's attitude seemed to stem from his oft-mentioned black belt in karate. There weren't too many times he went out drinking when he didn't find a chance to bring it up with somebody who was behaving badly, and he regaled us with these stories at work the next day. Usually, the other guy backed down, but sometimes Hank had to beat the concession out of him.

"Thanks," the manager said. He face was tight with stress. "How late are you guys going to work?" He was talking about the crew of six painters who had invaded his supermarket this evening.

"Probably two or three in the morning," Hank said. "We've got to spray the ceiling. Can't do it during the day, too many people around."

"Yeah, I know," the manager said. "It's just that the carpenters and floor guys were here all day making a mess, and now apparently you guys are going to work all night. We don't get a break." The grocery store was open 24/7.

Hank nodded. "Ever think about just closing the place down until the job is done?"

"Can't do that," the manager said quickly. "The remodel is going to take too long. Our regular customers would switch stores and never come back."

Hank wiped his finger through some construction dust on a food bin. "How about if they get dirty food?" he said. "Won't that make them switch stores too?"

"It's much less likely," the manager said, and he scuttled away to the sound of Hank's laughter.

..

Gary was a gambler. Between ten and midnight he'd often disappear from the grocery store and sneak across the street to a casino to try his luck on the video poker and keno machines.

Gary was also the crew foreman, the "lead" painter who was in charge when Mitch, the owner, wasn't around. Gary was a good painter whose services were much sought after by local contractors, but he did not come without liabilities; in addition to his gambling problem, he also had a once-yearly habit of "lying down," as he called it, which meant he would stop showing up for work and go through a period of doing drugs and heavy drinking. Usually these lie-downs lasted about a month; then he got back up and resumed normal life.

But even when he was standing, Gary was a gambler,

and whenever Mitch left on an errand Gary would hatch the same plan: make sure everybody has clear instructions and enough work to last an hour, then disappear. He would return red faced and talking fast, offhandedly spinning a fib about where he'd been. You could almost feel his heart thumping through his white painting shirt, mashing up a potent mix of adrenaline and shame.

Gary was small, about five feet tall, but he enhanced his puniness with long, red hair and a wide, red mustache that curled up at the ends. He was in his early forties, married with two young daughters and also caring for a teenage girl whose mom had died. "Her dad's a loser" was all he said about that. So while Gary blew a lot of money gambling, and his lie-downs put a lot of strain on his marriage, he did have a gentle, generous manner, and his wife, Lori, had gazed at him adoringly on the few occasions I'd seen them together— whenever she wasn't rolling her eyes.

Gary liked to gossip while we worked. "Hank's been waiting on that settlement for eight years now," he told me. "Problem is, the statute of limitations ran out after *seven* years. His own law firm let it expire on him." He laughed. "Fucking idiot."

He cleared his throat and got serious again; after all, he and Hank had been friends since high school. "I think those lawyers were on the take from the nail-gun company. Bastards kept giving Hank money when he needed it, telling him they were waiting for things to happen, waiting on motions and shit. . . . They'd give him a thousand here, a thousand there when he needed it. But then one day, they just stopped calling him. That's when he found out it was too late for him to collect. Assholes." It was clear Gary sided with Hank over the lawyers.

"But now," Gary said, triumph in his tone, "a federal judge is going to reopen the case. There's a law against getting screwed by your own lawyers like that, so they're going to take another look at it."

But soon the idea of Hank triumphing over corporate America vanished back into the darkness of reality. "He'll never get shit, though. They'll just keep dragging him along forever. Oh, well." Gary sounded sympathetic, as if he were being dragged along too, but it didn't seem to bother him much. That's just how Gary rolled.

..

Mitch, the owner of the company, was a material man. That's what Gary said—Mitch really knew his material. A good painter like Gary respected that knowledge, because good painters know it isn't easy to keep material straight.

Material is paint, simply put, but *paint* is a deficient word to describe the extensive selection of coatings manufactured for residential, commercial, and industrial paint jobs, designed for a thousand different purposes. An in-depth cross-brand knowledge of all these products is rare, so much so that other painting contractors often called Mitch with questions about what best to use in a tricky situation. Even the managers of local paint stores occasionally consulted Mitch about the supplies they were selling in their own stores. That says a lot when you consider the long-standing feud between painters and paint store managers over who knows more about paint and painting.

Mitch liked to downplay his knowledgeable reputation by saying, "Everything you need to know about painting you can read on the back of a paint can." But his training really was extensive, going all the way back to his Navy days, when he'd served an apprenticeship as an industrial painter. After his military stint, he'd spent fifteen years doing mostly commercial work, eventually starting his own company, which he had run for the past ten years somewhat successfully despite bankruptcy, divorce, and alcoholism during the same time period. Now his divorce was settled, he was dry, and he'd landed the biggest painting contract in town, the remodeling of several chain grocery stores. "Mitch is back," Gary liked to say when we'd pull up to the stores in our smart new work vans. "And everybody in this town knows it."

Although Mitch had all the material sorted out in his head, he also had a lot of other things mixed up in there, perhaps because he refused to wear a respirator and thirty-five years of paint fumes from all that different material he knew so much about had eroded his brain and given him a dyslexic style of speaking, especially when giving instructions. The crew was often left on the job thoroughly confused about what he really wanted done, resulting in costly mistakes. When that happened, Mitch turned into a sulking bull. He'd stomp around in silence until he could find a way to take it out on Kelly, his nineteen-year-old son from his broken marriage. More than once I saw him make Kelly cry.

..

Kelly was a born-again Christian. Exactly how that transformation took place at such a young age was a mystery because nobody in his family was religious, but everything about Kelly was confused like that. Kelly did things like drive to Kansas in pursuit of a sixteen-year-old love interest, fall asleep at the wheel somewhere in Colorado on the way, and total his Camaro. When he returned home in shame after that incident, showing up at the shop and avoiding all eye contact, Mitch yelled at him right there in front of us, telling Kelly he'd have to work it off, every penny. Kelly got teary and said he was sorry.

Later that night at the grocery store, though, Kelly told us the story of his Kansas adventure. We all laughed, and even Mitch smiled as Kelly blamed it all on the girl.

"Why do women play with men's hearts like that?" he asked his dad. We were sitting in a circle on the grocery store floor, taking our break in the soup aisle.

Mitch chuckled. "Just wait until you come home from work and find your wife fucking your best friend on the kitchen table. *Then* tell me about women."

Everybody looked at Kelly—after all, that was his mom on the table—but he laughed too, having heard the story many times before.

Mitch folded his hands behind his head and stretched out on the dusty floor, looking up at the ceiling. "Bastard was out of a job, so I let him live at my house. That's what you get when you do a buddy a favor. He starts screwing your wife while you're at work." He turned his head to Kelly. "You don't yet know much about women, son."

"I know my mom's a thief!" Kelly said, suddenly hot. Mitch looked away. Ten years after the divorce, he'd gotten slapped with a court order to pay years of back child support for Kelly's sister, who lived with his ex-wife. Mitch claimed they had agreed to raise one child each, thus evenly splitting the financial responsibilities, but he never got it in writing and paid dearly. The court placed a lien against all his assets and future earnings, and Mitch, who was remarried by then and on the verge of expanding his painting business, was shoved backward financially so far that he plunged anew into the depths of his old nemesis, alcohol. The episode almost cost him his second wife, a nice, pretty young woman he was lucky to have.

The story had a happy ending, though, because one day Mitch's new wife unloaded on his ex-wife's face in the Town & Country Lounge, punched her so hard she hit the floor. That sincere display of love and devotion spurred Mitch to turn his life around once again. Now he was back, and every painting company in town knew it.

..

Fred was an asshole with an ever-running mouth.

"Mitch is a loser," he informed me later. "He ate her shit for years while she fucked around. Ask any painter in town, anybody in construction, they'll tell you."

I didn't respond. Fred and I were prepping a section of

ceiling, driving around on an electric man-lift, spraying water marks with an aerosol can of oil-based stain-blocking primer. At the same time, we were caulking cracks in the ceiling's huge, wood-laminate support beams. There were about twenty of these beams, and each one spanned the entire store. Between the stains and the beams, we weren't moving too fast—we often had to wait for late-night shoppers to get out of our way—and Fred had long ago demonstrated a propensity for filling the dead air of the grocery store graveyard shifts with his arrogant and insincere commentary about himself and everybody else—except, of course, the person he was talking to. That would come later.

"Mitch thinks he's a big man now, but he'll fuck up again. He'll start drinking, I guarantee it."

I didn't answer.

"And his kid Kelly's a fucking idiot, isn't he? Man, that kid must have been dropped on his head or something when he was little." He paused. "What the fuck was he crying about the other day, anyway? I didn't hear Mitch screaming at him."

The other day Kelly and I were taping off some freezer doors when he told me his mom had bought a new horse trailer for his sister so she could ride on the high school rodeo team—bought it with money "stolen" from Mitch, which was the same thing as stealing from him. After this accusation he broke into tears and told me his mom hated him. I said no she doesn't, your mom doesn't hate you. "I know she doesn't love me," he said, and then he really started bawling, and that's when Fred happened to walk by and see us.

"Did he give you the God talk yet?" Fred continued, not really caring what Kelly was crying about. "Try to save you with that religious bullshit of his? Tried to do it to me one day and I told him to shut the fuck up. That church shit has him brainwashed. And it's all because of that chick, the one he chased to Kansas. She's the one who got him into that church, and now she's gone and he's still brainwashed. Everything about that kid is so fucked up, isn't it? He's so dense."

I shut him out and kept working. Eventually, Fred decided it was time to go call his girlfriend. He looked around for Gary, who we both knew was across the street gambling, and then instructed me to lower the man-lift and let him off. He headed for the pay phone at the back of the store.

I raised the lift, relieved to be alone, thinking what a hypocrite that guy is. He just met this girl a few weeks ago, but he couldn't go a single shift without calling her five times. Talk about brainwashed.

..

Hank announced he was finally going to get his money.

"No shit?" Gary said. "You're going to get it?"

Hank smiled and nodded. "Talked to my lawyer yesterday. Should be coming in about three weeks, maybe a month."

We were gathered in the parking lot of the paint shop, a warehouse space Mitch rented where he could spray a hundred doors at a time or five thousand feet of trim. We met at Mitch's shop every evening to load up the vans and have a crew meeting before heading to the grocery store.

"How much are you going to get?" Fred the asshole asked. Hank gave him a stony smile. "We're working on that."

"About how much?"

Hank still smiled, but we all knew Fred better shut up. And Fred did shut up, until later, when Hank wasn't around but the rest of the crew was.

"He's never going to get any money, I guarantee it. Haven't we heard this before? It's always two weeks, two months, I'm going to get my money. When's the guy going to realize they're just fucking with him? He's never going to get anything."

"Come on, Fred," Kelly said, shifting into the goofily optimistic demeanor he sometimes adopted to split time with his more desperate displays of emotion. "He might get something."

"He'll never get shit," Gary said, agreeing with Fred. The four of us were applying blue tape to a lengthy wall to create the multicolored, striped design the grocery store wanted. Now Gary stepped back and viewed our work, then peered again at a set of plans for the remodel. "Fred, are you sure we're doing this right?"

"Sure I'm sure." It was Fred's interpretation of the plans we were following. Mitch had explained the design scheme to us before he left on errands, but as usual nobody could understand what he was talking about. Finally, Fred grabbed the plans and began instructing us on how high and how wide each stripe should be and what color went where. An hour later we were ready to start painting, which seemed unwise in light of our confusion.

We had nothing else to do, though, so paint we did, a pastel array of orange and blue and yellow and tan and green, alternating between stripes to allow for dry time.

Four hours later we were done, right about the time Mitch showed up. He stared at the wall. "What the hell is this?"

Gary dropped his mouth. "We—" Desperately he looked around for Fred, then remembered Fred had disappeared a few minutes ago to go call his girlfriend.

Mitch turned to Kelly. "Did you tell them to do this?"

"Me? No, Dad . . ."

"Didn't you hear what I said when I left? I said the *blue* goes there and the *orange* goes there and the *brown* goes there and the *green* goes there." He was waving his arms wildly.

"Dad, we—"

"God damn it, Kelly," Mitch shouted. "You guys have wasted four hours of my time. Do you know how much it costs to pay four painters for four hours and have them fuck everything up? This comes straight out of my pocket."

"Dad, I—"

"Dad nothing," Mitch said. "Don't pull that Dad crap on me, Kelly. Not now."

Mitch stormed off. Kelly turned away, his face breaking. Gary, as lead painter, knew it should have been him getting reamed, and he put his arm around Kelly. "It's okay. It's not your fault."

Fred chose that moment to reappear. "Guess what?" he said. "I'm getting married."

..

Fred had found a good woman.

"Not everybody is lucky enough to find a good woman," he said. He looked at me. "You got a good woman?"

"No." I silently cursed Mitch for always assigning me to work with Fred. Tonight we were again motoring the manlift down an aisle, caulking cracks in the beams and spraying stain-killer on the ceiling, the never-ending ceiling. You just don't know how big a grocery store is until you paint the ceiling.

"Well, you should get one," he said. "Makes a big difference, you know. That's why I'm getting married so fast. When you find a good woman, you've got to grab her." With that he scanned the store below us for any sign of Mitch or Gary. "Hey, take me down."

I took him down. Fred hurried away, but in a couple minutes he was back, ordering me to come down and get him. He spoke in the same aggravated, clipped tone he always had after one of these missed connections. He would remain that way until the next attempt, and then the next, until he finally got hold of his fiancée. Then he'd be happy the rest of the night.

..

Gary blacked out from gambling. He told me about it as we sprayed a finish coat of paint on the ceiling one night.

"Had $1,200 in my pocket," he said. "Twelve one-hundred-dollar bills. And I remember sitting down at a poker machine and feeding the first one in . . ." He mimed that feeding motion, the so-familiar sliding of the fingers forward, then drew back a breath. "And that's the last thing I remember. When I woke up, the money was gone and I was just sitting there." He shook his head. "I know it sounds crazy, but it's true. I completely blacked out."

He lifted the four-foot spray wand and started shooting the ceiling. When he finished everything within reach, he lowered the wand and waited for me to maneuver the man-lift to the next section.

"I remember how my wife cried when I came home and told her. She knew how much we needed that money, there's no way I could hide it, so I just said, Lori, I lost the money. I blacked out." He looked down. "She didn't even yell at me or anything. She just cried."

He paused as he recalled the pain. "I thought, oh man, I really fucked up, she's going to leave me now. But she didn't. She got over it. And I went out and made some more money, and we were all right." He sounded proud she'd stuck with him. "Hell, I've always been able to make money—that's not the problem. It's hanging onto it that's the problem." He laughed. Life was good.

..

Fred committed suicide. He shot himself quick and simple in his parents' basement the weekend before his supposed wedding.

"He left a note," Mitch said. "To his fiancée. It sounds like they were having problems." He cleared his throat. "It's a sad thing."

It was 7 p.m. Sunday evening. We were gathered at the paint shop to start another week of work. We stood in a circle in the gravel parking lot in the fading light, same as we did every night, except tonight there was no Fred.

"But why did he have to kill himself?" Kelly asked, sounding bewildered. "He just met her a couple months ago. Why were they getting married so fast? I mean . . ."

Mitch put a hand on his shoulder. "I can't make sense of it either, son. I didn't know Fred that well, and I never met his fiancée."

"She probably started fucking around on him," Hank said.

Mitch narrowed his eyes. "Did he tell you that?"

"No," Hank said, "but that's what happens when you work the night shift. The woman is home alone every night and she resents it, starts fucking around. I've seen it happen to other guys who worked the night shift."

Mitch sighed. "It's a bad thing to be absent from a relationship, I know that." He looked at Kelly. "I was gone from my marriage, son, working all the time back in those days. That's why your mother did what she did. A lot of it was my fault."

"No, it wasn't," Kelly said, grabbing his father's arm. "Dad. It wasn't." They exchanged a look of longing for their lost family life.

Hank turned to Mitch. "This night-shift stuff is fucked, Mitch. We're painters. We're supposed to work during the day." He walked to a dark corner of the lot to stand by himself. Hank never had much use for Fred, but he could relate to having a hole in your head.

"We'll be done with the night shifts soon, guys, I promise," Mitch said, but a gloomy subtext lingered: if Fred could have made it just a few more weeks, maybe things would have worked out differently. Instead, Fred was dead.

..

That night Mitch took us all out to dinner. Not because Fred was dead—Mitch took us out to dinner almost every night around eleven or twelve. Usually, we piled into a paint van and drove together to a nearby twenty-four-hour restaurant. Mitch would pay for our food and the time it took to eat it, never signing us out, a generous deal from a man who, despite his occasional outbursts, was really a giver at heart. In addition to the nightly meal, every once in a while he'd slip a $50 bill into your hand and say, "Thanks for helping me make this work." Not all bosses think to do that.

Tonight the hostess seated us at our usual round table. Hank picked up Fred's chair and set it to the side to make more room for himself. We talked a lot, but not about Fred. Mitch joked with Kelly as we waited for our food. Kelly giggled in his goofy way and leaned over into his dad. Mitch started telling stories about his son's screw-ups, and we laughed. Gary had heard all these stories, but he knew I hadn't.

"Mitch, tell the one about the candy store," he said. Then he leaned over to me. "You gotta hear this."

Mitch laughed. "Oh, Christ, that was a long time ago."

"Dad, don't say *Christ*. That's a sin."

"Christ Christ Christ, how's that?" Mitch said, and Kelly punched him.

"Dad!"

"Son, you and your God stuff," Mitch said, shaking his head and grinning at how his clueless nineteen-year-old kid had become a born-again Christian.

"'Thou shalt not take the Lord's name in vain,'" Kelly quoted, but he was laughing too.

"Come on, Mitch, tell the one about the candy store," Gary prodded.

"Okay," Mitch said. "Well, this was about fifteen years ago when the big mall was being built. I'd landed the contract to paint the place."

Gary nudged me with his elbow. "Son of a bitch painted the whole mall by himself."

Mitch smiled, embarrassed. "It was right after the divorce," he said, "so I just lived at the job site. I had a sleeping bag and a mattress and I just slept right there, with Kelly next to me." He looked at his son. "I think you were four years old. Got to spend the summer living on a goddamn construction site." He chuckled.

"I remember, Dad. I thought it was fun."

"Anyway," Mitch said, "on the last day before the mall was supposed to open for business, I was still running around doing touch-up. The store owners were getting their shops set up, and everybody was in everybody's way, and somehow I lost track of Kelly. He ran off when I was doing something, I don't even remember what."

"This is so funny," Gary said, nudging me again. "Listen."

"When I realized he was gone I was like, Oh no, where the hell did that boy go? I started walking around the mall, yelling for him. Finally, I found him, and guess where he was? Little rascal had climbed into one of the big candy bins at the candy store and was sitting in there stuffing his face." Mitch chuckled. "He was crouched in the candy store display case like a monkey, grinning ear to ear."

Everybody laughed and looked at Kelly. He could do it tomorrow and we wouldn't be surprised.

The crew sat at the table for another hour telling stories. We didn't know it then, but in the coming years Mitch would overextend his business, go bankrupt, and collapse back into alcoholism, then get dry again and remake his business specializing in traditional plaster work—and his wife stuck with him the whole time. Kelly would join the Army, get kicked out, and return home in disgrace, then years later join his father in the plaster business—along with his sister. Gary would lie down with a more destructive drug than he'd ever done before, but he would pull out of it and his marriage would endure. As for Hank, he continued to wait for his nail gun money, but it never came. All he ever had was that picture of his brain.

But tonight we were a content crew of painters as we left the restaurant and climbed into the van to ride back to the job. Kelly jumped into the driver's seat, Mitch sat in the passenger seat, and the rest of us tried to arrange ourselves among the paint cans stacked in back. Kelly started the van and hit the gas before we got seated, then slammed on the brakes. He laughed as we fell over and the heavy cans tumbled around us.

"Goddamn it, Kelly," Mitch said. "You better not spill any of that material."

"Don't swear, Dad. Praise the Lord."

"Shut the hell up, son," Mitch said, but he was grinning as we pulled out of the parking lot. From my bucket seat in the back of the van, I listened to their teasing and tried to picture the two of them living together on a construction site for months, Mitch working all day while Kelly tagged along, then sleeping side-by-side on a mattress on the floor each night. I thought about my own father, a great dad but a man whose job always remained a mystery to me. He wore a suit and worked downtown, did something with insurance and investments and who the hell knows. It seemed strange, right then, that I didn't know. I thought maybe I should ask him before he dies.

6

risk takers

The phone call from Slater made me sit up on the couch. Slater was one of the biggest painting contractors in the Northwest, running crews all over Montana, Idaho, and eastern Washington while hosting up to one hundred painters on his payroll. His willingness to take on any job no matter the risks or complications was renowned in local construction circles, and the fact that he was contacting me personally was something of an honor—albeit a mixed one. Slater tended to skimp on safety, and having him on the phone could only mean hazardous times ahead.

"You're a rock climber, right?"

"Yes."

"Good," he said, "because I've got some high work for you."

..

"So do you think you can do it?" he shouted. It was later that afternoon, and we were standing on an iron catwalk seven stories off the floor of a massive building at the pulp mill west of Missoula, surrounded by stupendous fiery cauldrons and the insane roar of mega-machinery. It was hard to imagine it was all in the name of quiet cardboard boxes.

"So what do you think?" Slater shouted again. He was always pushing like that, and I swallowed a dry breath of trepidation. Slater was legendary not only for tackling hard jobs but also for blowing them up in spectacular fashion. Sometimes he deliberately cut corners in a quest to maximize profits; sometimes he just succumbed to his nature of popping off rounds without sighting down the barrel.

Once he'd ordered his crew to paint the floor of a military airplane hangar the wrong color, even though he knew it was the wrong color—he was impatient to get it done, and the ultra-durable material specified for the floor was not immediately available in quantities sufficient to get the correct color. He ended up having to strip and repaint the entire hangar floor, a giant headache that cost him fifty grand. Another time he got caught neglecting to strip the lead paint off hundreds of wood windows on a state government building, as was required by the expensive contract he'd won. Government engineers didn't discover the scam until final inspection, and they forced him to remove each and every window, take it to his shop, and strip it properly while the inspectors watched.

These were not isolated incidents, and as a result Slater was constantly cranked to maximum stress, pushing his crews and devising new ways to beat the system and make more money. Somehow—to everybody's astonishment—he'd managed to keep the whole crazy show rolling going on ten years now.

As for me, I'd participated in two Slater debacles. Once he paid me to spend several weeks painting below-ground sewage pipes at Missoula's wastewater treatment plant. I had followed his instructions precisely, but on my final day an inspector showed up and saw me spraying the last twenty feet of pipe. He fired a series of questions at me about how the pipes had been prepped—or not—and I told him to talk to Slater. The end result was that all the pipes had to be sandblasted and repainted the proper way. Slater had to eat the cost.

Another time I'd been on one of Slater's crews painting the barracks at a local military installation. About halfway through the job an inspector showed up, examined our bucket trucks, and immediately shut us down. He claimed every single boom showed signs of stress fractures, which didn't surprise the crew because Slater bought his bucket trucks well used and never did maintenance. As I said, safety was one of Slater's most common ways to skimp.

I suspected that was exactly what he had in mind at the pulp mill. We both knew high work like this was regulated by strict OSHA rules requiring hanging scaffolding and extensive backup safety systems, equipment that took many hours to rig and slowed jobs to a profit-eroding pace. That's what he was getting paid for—months and months of work—but he wanted me to slip in and out in three weeks using my lithe rock climbing gear, hopefully before anybody could figure out what was going on. He'd make a nice cache of cash if everything went as planned.

"So do you think you can do it?" he shouted again.

"Yeah, I can do it." Fact was, I needed a cache too.

"Using your climbing equipment?"

I nodded. "I'll need a partner to belay with." I pointed to the steel support beams near the ceiling. "We can walk on those beams to paint the ceiling, then rappel off the beams to spray the walls."

"How long are your ropes?"

"Hundred and fifty feet." We looked down at the cement floor seven stories below. Some mill employees were walking through, and the tops of their hard hats looked like gumdrops. "Should be long enough."

"Will it be safe?" He looked away. "I don't want anybody getting hurt."

"It will be about as safe as rock climbing, I guess."

He nodded quickly, uncertain exactly what that meant but satisfied I'd accepted responsibility for my own welfare—I was the rock climber, not him, and he was going to pay me an above-average wage for this work. "Know anybody who can help you? Somebody to—what did you call it—belay you?"

I nodded, and my mood improved. I knew somebody all right, my friend Thorn, a New Jersey creation and self-described "lowbagger" who'd moved to Montana a few years before and was a bit like me in that he'd graduated from college to become a ski bum—or in his case a snowboard bum—and he painted to support that lifestyle. Thorn liked hard jobs; in fact, he loved them. He never gave up and he never backed down, even if the job was only to get a cup of "cawfee" for his workmates at break time. How many of you want one, he'd ask. You? You? You? Then he'd fill the cups and deliver the drinks, not stopping until everybody was served. When he was satisfied he hadn't shirked a duty, he'd pour himself a cup and sit down to tell stories about his low-bagging adventures. Thorn was good at telling stories like this one.

··

"The whole thing started when my friend came over to my house and offered me a job."

"He came over to your house?"

Thorn cleared his throat. "Well, not exactly my 'house.' I was living in an old potato-chip truck at the time. You know, those big, boxy trucks with snacks painted on the side? It didn't run. It wasn't even mine. It belonged to some guy who moved away and left me the keys, and I needed a place to live, ya know? So I moved in. It was pretty sweet, actually. I had it parked in a hidden spot near the tracks on the north side of town."

"Sounds wonderful."

"Yeah," Thorn said. "Anyway, I was kind of broke at the time—"

"No."

"—and my friend said he'd been offered a job painting the inside of a paper mill, and he needed help. He said the job would require ropes and climbing gear, stuff I knew about because I've done some rock climbing. He made it sound like it would be sort of fun, kind of an adventure. And the pay was pretty good." Thorn furrowed his eyebrows under his buzz-cut brown hair. "Although by the end of the job the pay didn't seem that great anymore."

"So your friend tricked you into taking the job?"

"He didn't *trick* me," Thorn said, annoyed at the suggestion he was a chump. "He just didn't tell me the whole story. He didn't tell me what the place was really like."

"What was it like?"

"It sucked," Thorn said. "It was the worst place I've ever worked. It was so loud you had to wear earplugs the whole time, or else your ears would be ringing when you got home at night, like after a rock concert, ya know? And on top of that there was all this crap floating in the air, wood particles and sawdust that got in your eyes all day long. I bet I rinsed my eyes a hundred times on that job, but I'd still go home every night with this sharp stuff in my eyes that never came out. It made it hard to sleep."

"In the potato-chip truck."

"Yeah."

"What about your friend? He must have got stuff in his eyes too, right?"

"He did, but right at the beginning he bought himself a good pair of safety goggles that worked a lot better than the cheap ones our boss gave us. So for him it wasn't really a problem."

"Why didn't you buy yourself some of those good goggles too?"

Thorn shrugged. "I was going to, but I just never did, ya know? I never got around to it."

"Oh."

"Anyway," Thorn said, "on our first day of work the boss showed us around the mill, and I was amazed at how loud and hot the place was, full of these big burning tanks and shit. That's when my friend decides to tell me there was a freakin' *explosion* in this building a year ago, and two people were seriously injured. He said we'd better do this job fast, because as long as we were working in this building we were living on 'borrowed time.' I was like, Dude, you didn't say anything about borrowed time when you asked me to do the job. But he just laughed, because he knew it was too late for me to back out."

"Wouldn't it be better to back out than get blown up?"

"Yeah, but once I start something, I don't quit until it's done. My friend knew that about me."

"Oh."

"And he also knew that I always volunteer to do the hard jobs, ya know? The things nobody else wants to do. And that's exactly what I ended up doing on this job—all the hard, dangerous stuff nobody else wanted to do."

"Such as?"

"Well, to start off, I had to pressure-wash the entire place while swinging from a crane cable."

"A crane cable?"

"Yeah, a cable system the mill had installed to lift equipment around inside the building. It was totally against the rules to hook a person to it, but the boss wanted to get the pressure-washing done as quickly as possible so we could start painting, and he asked if any of us would be willing to hang from the cable."

"And you volunteered."

"Of course I did. That's just the way I am, ya know? But about ten minutes into the job I wished I didn't volunteer, because every time I'd spray a wall the force of the water would spin me around in circles. After a while I started to feel sick. And then my legs fell asleep in my harness and they stayed that way all day, and I was covered in all this gross greasy shit and completely soaked too."

"That must have been one long day."

"You don't even know. And to top it all off, those guys kept fucking with the cable controls and jerking me around on purpose because they thought it was funny."

"Those guys?"

"Yeah, my friend and this other guy we were working with, an ex-con with a teardrop tattoo below his eye, like he'd killed somebody, you know? He ran the controls on the cable all day, and he kept jerking me around on purpose."

"So your friend didn't actually jerk you around."

"No, but he didn't stop the guy."

"Maybe he didn't want to get murdered."

"Whatever," Thorn said. "If it had been me, I would have stopped the guy."

"Okay, so your friend should have stopped the guy."

"Yeah," Thorn said, briefly satisfied but then frowning

again. "And he could have stuck up for me the next day too, when we started painting the ceiling."

"How so?"

"Well, our boss Slater was there, and that made me kind of nervous, ya know? He was a big guy who yelled a lot—I mean we all had to yell because the place was so loud, but he really screamed at me."

"What was he screaming at you about?"

"First he was screaming that I should walk faster on the beams. He said we'd never get done if I went so slow. But I was scared, ya know? It was my first time walking on the beams. I was clipped into our safety ropes and everything, but it was still scary the first time. The floor was way the fuck down there."

"Did Slater yell at your friend too?"

Thorn shook his head. "My friend was just watching, standing with Slater on a catwalk. He'd worked for Slater before, so they sort of knew each other. They were trying to figure out a system, and they were using me as a guinea pig on the first section. I volunteered to do it, though."

"Of course. So what happened?"

"When I finally got out to where I was supposed to start painting, my spray gun wouldn't work. I had no idea what was wrong with it, but I didn't want to walk back on the beams because the boss was yelling at me to hurry up. So I tried to take the gun apart to see if I could fix it, but my hands were shaking and I dropped some pieces."

"Dropped them? How far?"

"Six stories or something, all the way to the floor. Luckily, nobody was down there. Of course, then Slater really started freaking out, yelling that those spray guns cost $100 apiece. And then he started screaming about how we had to spray all the paint we'd mixed within ninety minutes, or the epoxy would harden and the paint would go to waste. He yelled that I was going to cost him $500—and all I was doing was standing out there on this friggin' ten-inch beam with no idea what to do."

"So what *did* you do?"

"The ex-con ran out to the truck and got me a different gun. It was an old shitty one that leaked all over my hands for the next three weeks, but I didn't complain because I felt bad about the one I dropped. I told the boss I'd pay for it, but he just yelled at me to get back out there and start painting. I did, and he stood there on the catwalk for the next hour and watched every move I made. And then all of a sudden, after he watches me paint this *entire* section, he starts screaming again!"

"What now?"

"I couldn't tell," Thorn said, his voice strained with exasperation, "because I couldn't hear him. I was a long ways out on these beams. I decided to go back to see what he was yelling about, and as I walked—just so it wouldn't seem like I was wasting time—I sprayed the tops of the beams behind me because I knew they had to be painted too. Slater screamed at me the entire time, getting madder and madder as I got closer to him, but I couldn't tell what the fuck he was saying.

"When I got to him he yelled that I forgot to paint a small

section of wall at the far end of where I'd been working. He said I had to go back out on the beams and do it, because we couldn't afford to leave any unpainted spots behind like that, we had to do everything while we had the safety ropes in place.

"And I'm like, Wait a minute, dude, I can't go back out there. I just painted the friggin' tops of all the beams, they're *wet*. And he just screams that I'd *better* get the fuck back out there and paint that wall or I'm fired. And I'm like, Wait, I can't even *reach* that wall from the beams, it's too far away—that's why I skipped it in the first place, ya know? There's no way to get it."

"I bet he loved that."

"Yeah," Thorn said. "So he points to this little pipe down below the beams and tells me I'm going to have to climb down onto the pipe to get that section. And I'm like You gotta be kidding me. You want me to climb onto that little pipe, this high off the ground? And he's like, Yep, you gotta do it."

"So did you?"

Thorn nodded. "I crawled back out there through the wet paint, lowered myself onto the little pipe, and stood on it while I sprayed that section. My shoes and hands were all slippery from wet paint, and I thought for sure I might fall."

"But even if you did fall, your safety rope would have caught you, right?"

"Normally, yeah, it would have."

"Normally?"

"I wasn't tied into it."

"Excuse me?"

"The rope wouldn't reach, so I had to untie to get down onto that pipe."

"Are you serious? You crawled down onto that little pipe without even being tied into the safety rope? Did your boss see you do that?"

"Yeah," Thorn said, "and so did my friend. They kind of laughed like I was crazy. But I didn't really mind, ya know? Because the boss respected me a lot more after that and didn't scream at me anymore. Between that and the pressure-washing, he could see I was doing all the hard jobs."

..

"Anyway, after a while we got into a routine," Thorn said. "Every morning my friend would pick me up at the potato-chip truck and we'd drive out to the mill. For two weeks this went on. Then all of a sudden one day he doesn't show up."

"He doesn't show up?"

"Yeah," Thorn said. "He just didn't show up one day when he was supposed to pick me up. And I was pissed because I had to walk up to the highway and hitchhike and it took me like an hour. It made me late."

"It seems strange that he just wouldn't show up."

"Yeah," Thorn said. "I couldn't believe it either."

"So when you got out to the mill, did you ask him why he didn't show up?"

"Not right away, because he wouldn't even talk to me. He acted like I didn't even exist. I started to work, but I got madder and madder. Finally, I stopped what I was doing and walked out on the beams to where he was spraying, and I'm like, What the fuck, dude, why didn't you pick me up this morning? You made me late."

"What did he say?"

"He said he didn't pick me up because I'm never ready when he comes. And I'm like, Oh God, not this again. Just because it takes me a few minutes to grab my stuff in the mornings, ya know? Like maybe ten minutes at the most."

"Ten minutes is a long time to make somebody wait every day."

"Oh come on, ten minutes, big deal. I didn't have an alarm clock, ya know? No electricity. Most days I didn't even wake up until he honked his horn. But once he honked, I got ready fast."

"Why didn't you just buy a battery-powered travel alarm clock? They're about five bucks at any convenience store."

"That's exactly what he said. And I was going to buy one, ya know? But I just never got around to it."

"Hmmm. So what happened then?"

"Well, after bitching at me about making him wait, he starts yelling at me about other stuff too. Just totally starts going off."

"About what?"

"First, he starts giving me crap because I took a few sips off his water bottle the other day. His precious little water bottle."

"You took a few sips?"

"Yeah, just a few sips, ya know? He always brought the water bottle up on the beams with us, and I was thirsty, the place was hot and dusty, and it took forever to get down off the beams and go to the drinking fountain. So I took a few sips off his water bottle once in a while. I guess he was mad because I finished all the water one day, and there wasn't anything left when he wanted a drink. But I figured he brought it up there for us to share, ya know? I didn't think he was going to hog it all for himself."

"Why didn't you just buy a water bottle of your own and bring it up there? You can get one at any convenience store. It costs about two dollars."

"Yeah, I was going to do that," Thorn said. "But I just never got around to it. Ya know?"

"Here's what I know, Thorn—you're a frickin' cheap bastard."

"That's exactly what he said! But I'm not cheap. I'm just a lowbagger—I gotta make every penny count. And I didn't really need any of those things, he just *thought* I needed them. And besides, I was the one doing all the hard jobs, ya know? I was the one that used the leaky spray gun and had paint running onto my hands all day, I was the one who got the respirator that hardly worked, and I was the one who walked the pipe and got swung around on the death cable to do the pressure-washing. I did all the things he didn't want to do. So he owed me a little water."

"Did you tell him that?"

"I did, and then he starts going off about how maybe I do the hard jobs, but I do them all wrong! And I'm like, You're kidding me, what the fuck are you talking about, wrong? I'm not doing anything wrong. And he's like, Oh yeah you are, you keep missing spots. And I'm like, Missing spots? What the fuck are you talking about, missing spots? And then he starts pointing out all these little tiny spots he says I missed, these teeny-tiny spots way up on the ceiling of this friggin' paper mill that nobody will ever see. I'm like, You're kidding me—those spots? And he's like, Yeah, those spots, and then he points to one nearby in a section I painted. And I'm like, *That* spot, is that what you're talking about? And he's like, Yeah, that's exactly what I'm talking about. So I grabbed his spray gun out of his hand and sprayed the spot. Except I didn't aim very well, and I sprayed him right in the face."

"You sprayed him right in the face?"

"By accident," Thorn said quickly, "right in the face. He'd taken off his goggles and respirator, so it went in his eyes too."

"Ouch, that must have hurt."

"Oh, yeah," Thorn said, looking down, "that industrial paint was really toxic. And I felt bad right away. I didn't mean to spray him in the eyes."

"So what did he do?"

"First, he yelled that he couldn't see. Then he started shuffling toward the catwalk, holding onto the beams. He had to unclip from the safety line to get around a support, and I thought he was going to fall, ya know? So I said, Here, let me help you, and I tried to grab his arm, but he shoved my hand away. And I'm like, *Here,* let me help you, and I grabbed him again, ya know? But when I did, one of his feet slipped off the beam, and he almost fell. I was like holy-shit-that-was-close. I didn't try to help him anymore after that."

"So did he make it?"

Thorn nodded. "Yeah, he made it eventually. He got down off the beams and cleaned the paint off his face, and at lunch we talked about it. We even laughed a little because it wasn't the first time we'd gotten pissed at each other about stupid stuff like this, but we always just apologized and moved on. He said he'd share his water with me, and I said I'd buy an alarm clock, and everything was cool.

"So did you buy an alarm clock?"

"No," Thorn said. "I never got around to it."

..

One day before we would have finished the job, the plant safety manager shut us down.

It didn't come as a huge surprise, because we'd noticed the way he and the other plant employees had started scrutinizing our methods. While we'd been painting the ceiling, it was hard for them to see us, but once we started painting the walls—rappelling off the beams on our climbing ropes— we inevitably had to make our way to ground level, where we came into clear view.

Obviously, our dinky climbing gear was not what they'd expected when they contracted this job out. They'd expected hanging scaffolding, elaborate riggings, full-on OSHA compliance. What they got was two climbing bums and an ex-con cranking through the job much faster than they'd imagined possible. They sensed something foul, and during our third week they started coming in to watch us more and more often, pointing fingers and talking while we pretended they weren't there. Finally, on the day we were doing our last series of rappels, the safety manager waved us down off our ropes and told us to leave the premises.

We didn't say a word. We just got in the van and left. We called Slater from a gas station. He sounded supremely disappointed that the job had been stymied just short of his ability to proclaim it complete and collect payment. But he'd wiggled out of tighter fixes than this, so he told us to go home and wait to hear from him.

The next day he called me from the mill. "Hey, can you and your buddy come out here and give these guys a demonstration? Just show them how you use your climbing gear, show them it's safe?"

I picked up Thorn and we drove out to the mill. Slater ushered us into a breakroom where a group of hard-hatted managers wore serious faces. Thorn and I put on a dog and pony show with the climbing gear, threw around a few technical terms, and assured the men that everything we were doing was perfectly safe or Lord knows we wouldn't be doing it. We even managed to say that last part without laughing.

When we were done the men conferred briefly, then the safety manager stood up and told us to go ahead and finish the job. "We've never had any rock climbers out here before," he added. Slater smiled, gave us a thumbs-up, and drove away in his truck, knowing he'd just pulled off one of the most lucrative painting coups of his life.

It was a life that lasted only ten more years. It's not hard to say what killed Slater at forty-eight: he drank himself to death. The official cause was "respiratory arrest" due to "acute alcohol pancrata." But I think it was the stress that really killed him, brought on by his thirst for gambling on big contracts and the constant barrage of self-inflicted debacles he had to overcome, and, almost worse, the occasional jackpot—like the paper mill—that only whet his ego for more. Eventually, I moved away from Missoula and didn't work for him anymore, but I did run into him a couple of times when I visited, and every time he looked more strung out and anxious, his manner one of almost obsessive distraction. He would take a minute to chat, but then he'd climb back in his big pickup truck and speed away to whatever screwed-up painting projects he had going on, whatever current catastrophes, be they in Spokane, Missoula, Bozeman, or Billings. He drove that truck hard through life. When he finally wrecked, it killed him.

As for Thorn, he's still lowbagging around somewhere.

7

fathers and daughters

As I entered my thirties, painting began to demoralize me. I'd inhaled more than my share of fumes from solvents proven to rot minds, along with far too much construction dust full of whatever carcinogens they'd developed to replace asbestos and lead. I wore respirators and dust masks more regularly than most painters, but there was no way to really keep out the noxious derivatives of the profession, and I started to fixate on the cumulative effect all these chemicals might be having on my mind and body. I worried about my eyes in particular, because they are the hardest to protect from the fine overspray mist that surrounds a painter much of the time. Goggles can be used in truly dire situations, but the lenses quickly get speckled with paint and are almost impossible to keep clean, making them impractical for daily use. My eyes had absorbed a lot of paint over the years, and the sensation of a chemical army invading through my soft and vulnerable eyeballs started to harry me. I had 20-20 vision, and the older I got the more I appreciated that fact. It seemed beyond stupid to risk screwing up my perfect eyes in the name of a mediocre paycheck.

And it wasn't just the physical downside that bothered me. For the first time in my life, I doubted myself. Being a twenty-something rock climber and skier had made it easy to view painting as a pit stop, but the attractiveness of that life faded quickly after thirty, and inevitably I started to wonder if I had anything else in the tank. The best-selling-novelist plan had stalled a few million dollars short of the finish line, and now I felt as if I was standing in the middle of the track while all the other cars whizzed by me on their way to success and fulfillment. I hadn't even finished college. I was a painter.

When a long-term relationship ended badly—she wanted kids and a future, imagine that—I finally decided to complete my degree, partly to show her but also to shake my own disappointment. I took the four remaining classes and then lined up an internship at an outdoor-sports magazine in Colorado. I spent several months in Boulder, editing at the magazine three days a week while painting the other two days for a local outfit that specialized in remodels. I returned to Montana, filled out my graduation papers, and received my diploma, thirteen years after first enrolling as a freshman. I never thought I'd care, but now that I was finally done I experienced a distinct sense of accomplishment. It felt good to finally throw that hat in the air.

When the hat came down, I started a painting company.

..

I didn't expect anybody to be thrilled about it. Nonetheless, the palpable disappointment exhibited by some people smarted. My parents, of course, were hoping I'd turned some sort of corner, and now apparently that notion was being spit back in their face. The publisher of the magazine where I'd worked said it sounded great when I told him on the phone. But keep writing, he added, in a way that implied I'd taken the wrong fork in the road. This belief in my ability didn't stop him from rejecting a story I sent him two months later, and I thought, Well, screw you too, buddy. Be a writer, sure, but who's going to pay the bills? Not you, and not my parents, and not anybody else who thinks I should be doing something more with my life. You come to Montana and try to find a better way to make a living than painting. People wipe their asses with master's degrees in Missoula, they work at convenience stores, and you're going to judge me for choosing $25 an hour instead of minimum wage? Who's the stupid one here?

My defiance, though, was just one of several facades I used to cope with my own discomfiture. I called my company "The Best Painter in the World" to show how witty and confident I could be—I'm the smartest stupid painter you'll ever meet, see? On my fliers I referred back to my College Craftsmen days and claimed that now, more than a decade later, I was returning to graduate school and was "back in business." It was a lie. I wasn't going to graduate school—I just couldn't admit (to people I didn't even know) that, ten years later, I was still painting.

I coped by pouring myself into the painting business. I specialized in doing superior work for high-end clients, perfect down to the smallest detail. I took out a Yellow Pages ad, designed trifold brochures, set up booths at home shows, and learned advanced faux-finishing techniques that make sponge-painting look like the kindergarten activity it is. I got in the best shape of my life too, because I'm telling you right now that if you set out to paint big houses by yourself one after another, it's a hell of a lot of work. From top to bottom and all the way around, everything is on you. That's exactly how I wanted it, though, because I was way too smart to hire any stupid painters. Even if the task was merely picking up paint chips from the flower bed at the end of a job, only one person can be the best.

..

Maybe my dedication was only to mask my dissatisfaction, but hard work has a way of generating good karma, and it was during this time that I met the girl I would eventually marry. She was a twenty-seven-year-old graduate student at the University of Montana who didn't seem to much notice that I was a thirty-something painter, which I thought a bit odd. But such nonjudgment can be the most powerful form of persuasion, and with her in my life I found myself more desirous than ever to break out of the painting trade. But how, when, where? I had no answers to these questions.

Then one day I was eating breakfast and reading the newspaper before work when I saw a classified ad seeking an editor of outdoor-recreation books in Helena, the capital city of Montana, about two hours from Missoula. I'd never seen such an ad before, had never really considered the possibility that such a cushy career might exist in a hard-scrabble place like Montana. A "real" job for somebody with a college degree who has extensive knowledge of outdoor sports? Holy crap, that's me. That's me right there.

I got the job, shut down my painting business, and, along with my wife-to-be, moved east across the Continental Divide to Helena. I'll never forget the overwhelming sense of release I experienced the first day I sat down behind a desk to start work. It was January, it was awful outside, but I didn't need to worry about the weather anymore. I didn't need to worry about fumes corroding my sensibilities, or lacquer mist eating my eyes, or dust clogging my air passages. After fifteen years of making money through muscle movement, now somebody was going to pay me to be sedentary. Unbelievable.

..

I luxuriated behind that desk for three wonderful years, but eventually, like a dormant virus, painting flared anew.

I'll never forget the day I pulled my old crumpled painter's pants out of the plastic bag where they'd been stored, along with my paint-speckled T-shirts, my paint-covered ball cap, and my paint-stiffened work shoes. I dumped it all on the floor, smelled the smells, and sighed. Thirty-six years old and tomorrow I'd be making money with my muscles again. They already ached.

My wife and I had just moved to Whidbey Island in Washington State, an atoll about two hours north of Seattle where she had accepted a new teaching job. The reasons we left Montana were several, but near the top of the list was that her teaching salary would rise more than 50 percent. And surprise of surprises, I was to become a teacher too; while working as an editor, I'd enrolled part-time at a local college and earned my teaching license. The only require-ment unmet was my student-teaching internship, which I was supposed to be getting ready to do right now, rather than painting.

But the move away from Montana had complicated the situation, and the student-teaching coordinator had failed to line up anything in Washington. Now she was trying to fix that, but in the meantime I found myself with nothing to do on an island where, much like Montana, the most obvious way to make a decent living was in construction. So back to painting it was, while I waited for this student-teaching deal to work itself out.

Except it wasn't that easy. I called five different contrac-tors and got no offers. All my years of one-call-for-work had spoiled me, and I was unaccustomed to such denial. My wife started teaching, and I puttered around the house feeling like a letch. Finally, I convinced the wife/business manager of one of the contractors to meet me at McDonalds for an interview. I brought a painting resume, talked the talk, showed her how clean and not addicted to crack I was. She said she'd tell her husband to "try me out," and I went home, relieved. A week later, no call. Two weeks later, still nothing, and I was too embarrassed to follow up. The fact that I couldn't even get a job as a painter was an unexpected low point in my life, just when I'd thought I was trending upward.

I persisted, though, and finally I did get a call from one of the contractors in town. In retrospect, the wait was worth it, because this is how I came to know the best painter in the world. Not the pretend best painter in the world—the real best painter in the world. A baby-faced twenty-seven-year-old whose skills were so sharp I ended up flushing much of my own fifteen years down the toilet and relearning from him. Wondering, all over again, how something as simple as painting could be so hard to do right.

..

The morning of my first day, Franklin asked if I would be coming back the next. He shrugged when I said of course.

"At least half the people Larry hires only work one day. Most of them are lowlifes and scumbags. I've seen hundreds of them come and go. Seriously, like a hundred." He stopped scraping the fence we were prepping and looked at me. "But you seem pretty normal, I guess. You'll probably be back."

"Thanks." It was odd to have a guy ten years my junior sizing me up before I'd known him an hour, but at least he was right.

"That's why I hate being a painter," Franklin said. "Too many drug addicts and lowlifes. When people learn you're a painter they think you're a lowlife too. You can tell by how they look at you."

I looked at him. His hair was stylishly combed; his face, smooth and handsome. He was about six feet tall and in top shape, with work-hardened biceps pressing against his short sleeves. He wore a clean T-shirt and clean blue jeans, rather than a paint-splattered shirt and painter's pants like me. Clearly he didn't want to be tagged as a lowlife any more than necessary.

He told me he'd been Larry's lead painter for eight years. "How long have you been painting?" he asked, sounding ready to compare. When I told him, he gave me a new look, seeming surprised at how old I obviously was. My face warmed as I explained that I had messed around a lot in my youth, climbing, skiing ... cool stuff like that.

"That sounds nice," he said with a sigh. Then, after a moment, "I never really had a 'youth.'" The comment seemed to overreach our brief acquaintance and left me with nothing to say, but I didn't need anything to say: for the rest of the day while we painted the fence (a lengthy barrier surrounding a horse pasture), Franklin told me about his childhood as a Navy brat with a drunken dad who regularly beat him and his mom; how at nineteen he married his pregnant girlfriend; how at twenty he got divorced, fought for custody, and won because his ex had plummeted into postpartum depression and wanted nothing to do with the child. Now he was twenty-seven and lived with his daughter in a trailer "underneath the planes," meaning in the flight paths of the radar-jamming jets that train in the skies above Whidbey Island Naval Air Station.

"I hate living there," he said. "The noise totally stresses me out."

I didn't ask him why he didn't move. My wife and I had carefully bought our house far away from those roaring, soaring monsters, but if our real-estate search had taught us one thing, it's that housing is much more affordable "underneath the planes."

"I swear they drop gas on us sometimes," he continued, indignant. "I can smell it. I called the base and told them to stop, but they said no, they didn't drop any gas. But here's the thing. They have to lose fuel weight before they can land. They claim it evaporates before it hits the ground, but I swear I smell it on my lawn. Fucking Squids don't care, though. They look down on anybody who isn't Navy. Especially if you're a local person and work in construction." He assessed me again with furrowed eyes. "They probably won't look down on you, though, because you're not from here. And plus, your wife is a teacher."

It seemed like a logical time to tell him that I was going to be a teacher too, and he nodded as if he'd known all along I wasn't a real painter, regardless of how long I'd been doing it. "Good, I'm glad for you," he said. "Go use your brain. I wish I could. Painting sucks."

Changing the subject, I asked him about his daughter and he smiled. "She's in second grade. She's the smartest kid in her class, the teacher told me. I put money away every month in a college-savings program. It comes straight out of my bank account so there's no way I can skip paying it. She's going to be successful, I can tell. She's a lot smarter than I ever was. I never paid attention in school." He waved his brush at the fence. "I guess that's why I have to do this."

..

All fall I waited for my student-teaching assignment to be lined up. At least once a week, Larry, the owner of the company, asked me when I was leaving. He'd already laid off the rest of the summer crew but kept me around at Franklin's request. As many times as I explained the situation, Larry would ask me again the next week. It's not that he didn't understand; by coincidence, his wife was a schoolteacher just like mine. It's just that he'd been jacked around by too many bullshitting painters over the years, lied to, and then left in the lurch. The way he looked right past me showed that he knew better than to trust a painter. When I arrived at the workshop behind his house each day at 8 a.m., his first words were never "Good morning" but instead a grunted order to load whatever ladders we needed onto the van. Then he would walk away without another word.

Franklin, on the other hand, talked to me constantly. He also asked me repeatedly when I was leaving, never really listening to the answer. "I guess I'll be back to working alone then," he would sigh. "Oh well, I've done it before. I remember one stretch when Larry made me work alone for two and a half years. It took him forever to hire somebody."

The fact that Larry would keep Franklin working alone for such a long stretch didn't surprise me, because Franklin's aggressive brand of craftsmanship made him worth three painters at least. He handled ladders like they were made of Styrofoam and cranked out entire houses in a day. I watched him closely and, over the course of several months, found myself adopting more and more of his streamlined methods and handy tricks to paint better and faster. Even using his methods, I had a hard time keeping up with Franklin because his default speed was twice mine—this despite the fact that I'm a faster painter than most.

Despite his tireless pace, Franklin retained a critical eye for superior results that effortlessly exceeded what I'd thought were my own high standards. He considered interior trim work to be his specialty, and he showed me several techniques to prep the wood that—along with his finely honed spraying skills—resulted in a silkier, smoother finish than I'd ever achieved. His multifaceted method for filling nail holes made them completely disappear, not almost disappear like most painters' nail holes. There is a difference.

And it wasn't just the nail holes; it was the joints too. I'd always considered myself an expert caulker, meticulous and fine lined and, quite frankly, legions better than anybody I'd ever met. But one day Franklin looked at a doorjamb I was caulking and referred to it as "rookie."

"Look at those," he said, pointing at the upper inside corners of the jam. "They're rounded."

"You're full of shit," I said, staring at the corners. I always pressed my finger deep into those corners when smoothing caulk, and any remaining "rounding" was purely speculative, in my opinion.

He shook his head. "Here, try this." He pulled a cotton swab out of his pocket and handed it to me. "Wet it, stick it in the corners, and you can make them perfectly square, the way they should be." He was right, of course, and never thereafter did I go painting without a few cotton swabs in my toolbox. It's not that I begrudged the tip; it's just that I'd always considered interior trim work to be *my* specialty—and here I was being taught new and superior methods by a guy who had been in second grade when I painted my first house.

One day Franklin laughed while he watched me work. Immediately insecure, I asked him what I was doing wrong this time.

"Nothing."

"Then what are you laughing at?"

"I was just thinking about how before Larry hired you, he showed me your resume and I saw "The Best Painter in the World" on there. I was like, Holy crap, the best painter in the world. This guy might try to take my job. I was worried." He paused before the punch line. "Until I saw you paint."

I laughed along with him, but the comment knifed into my pride. Franklin knew I was a good painter, probably the best he'd ever worked with. But the college boy had to be put in his place, had to acknowledge the truly gifted one among us. Was I gifted at anything? Probably not from Franklin's perspective, though he nonetheless coveted my education and hardly disguised that fact. He told me numerous times about how he'd taken some community college classes one semester. He clung to that semester, to those few classes, in his mind as he disparaged the painting life out loud. I guess that's what prevented me from making fun when he referred to Minneapolis as a state and made other conversational missteps. I suppose having an education made it tolerable for me to stand down and let him teach me how to paint, but it didn't really work the other way around.

So Franklin's needling, like all needling, was rooted in insecurity, and the fact that I didn't want his $18-an-hour foreman job was one more reason for him to keep me around. Most of the painters bristled at Franklin's attempts to teach them new methods, and occasionally they even tried to bad-mouth him behind his back, to convince Larry that Franklin wasn't such a great painter after all. (Larry, whether or not he believed these lies, seemed to delight in presenting these accusations to Franklin and keeping him on edge—after eight years of working together, they were deeply enmeshed in all kinds of mind games.) But to Franklin, the fact that I ungrudgingly adopted his methods meant I admired his painting and would never bad-mouth him to Larry. And he was right about that. I would never bad-mouth him to Larry.

Finally, in early December, my student-teaching supervisor informed me she had a slot lined up starting after Christmas vacation. I gave Larry notice, and two weeks later I said good-bye and drove away from the shop, leaving Larry and Franklin standing outside watching me go. I was just another painter who had passed through their lives, unusual only in that I was leaving on good terms and also leaving the profession altogether. That was something they didn't see every day.

..

A month later I was back. The student-teaching assignment had fallen through, and I needed work. Larry started me the day after I phoned, but I could tell he was suspicious. Was I just another jerk-painter jacking him around? Was I really going to be a teacher, or did I just want a month off to binge? I repeatedly explained the difficult circumstances of my Montana student-teaching coordinator trying to line up an assignment in Washington, but I could tell he was trying to read my eyes more than listen. Most painters can't be trusted, that much he knew.

Franklin, for his part, was relieved to see me back. His long, lonely winter sentence had been granted a reprieve. He was almost giddy as we drove to the first job together in the van. He ran through all the evocative theories he entertained about Larry's private life, and his hyperbole escalated as I laughed and nodded even though I didn't believe most of it. As much as I did not want to be back painting, I did realize, after a month away, how much I liked working with Franklin. His mind was always running out loud, and it seemed to take an adventurous course most of the time.

When April rolled around, I resigned myself to the fact

that I wasn't going to get a student-teaching assignment that year but would have to wait until the next fall. I was just starting to accept my fate—six more months of painting, I can do that—when my phone rang early one morning. I assumed it was Larry—he called most mornings to make sure I was still alive or something—but it wasn't Larry. It was my teaching coordinator. She'd found a nearby high school willing to take me on for the last two months of the school year. Could I attend a meeting today—like right now, this morning—with the teacher and then start Monday? She noted that it would be an abbreviated internship, but she was willing to approve it because she felt bad for the delay.

After hanging up I stood in the kitchen, looking at my packed lunchbox and my rain gear in a bag next to it. Larry wanted me to pressure-wash a house that day. I wondered how many houses I'd pressure-washed over the years . . . hundreds. God, how I hated pressure-washing. Hated the bleach in my eyes, the water down my back, the cold soaking I always got no matter how much waterproof gear I wore. Monday morning I'd be walking through the halls of a high school, trying not to get trampled by teenage apathy and disrespect—and it sounded absolutely delightful. I was so ready to not pressure-wash that house.

I called Larry and gave him the news. "That's great," he said, sounding, more than anything, pleased that he'd been right to stick with me.

"So I guess this means I can't wash the house."

"Forget the house—I'll have Franklin do it. You focus on your new career. That's what's important."

"Thanks for everything, Larry," I said, and we hung up. I took a deep breath and did exactly as Larry said: focused on my new career. If everything went as planned, painting would be part of my past.

..

Two months later I was back. But only because it was summer, and I needed to earn some extra cash. Great, Larry said when I called, we can use you. Franklin, too, was glad to have me on the crew to offset some of the other clowns Larry had signed up for the summer. But I made it clear to Larry and Franklin that I'd been hired to teach next fall at the high school where I'd done my practicum, so I wouldn't be around long. Way to go, they said. You must have made a good impression if they hired you. We're glad it all worked out.

At the end of August we parted ways for a third time. Franklin didn't say much because he knew I was truly moving on to a new profession now, and this time it was for real. Larry, who had warmed to me considerably over the summer now that he knew I wasn't a fraud, told me with a gruff smile to Get the hell out of here and don't ever come back again. All right, I said, laughing. This time I'm gone for good.

..

A year later I was back.

The high school laid me off due to declining enrollment.

There was no debating the teachers' contract stipulation. I had only one year of seniority, so I was out, along with a few other folks low on the post.

And of all the times I had returned to painting, this proved the hardest. At thirty-eight years old, almost thirty-nine, I was starting to feel my life's lot settling around me surreptitiously but unmistakably—the quicksand that is mortality. Being back in a dropout occupation and looking forty in the face made me acutely aware that the future presented fewer options and more obstacles. Having to pick up the phone and ask Larry for work—again—made me wonder, in the simplest of terms, What in the world am I going to do with my life? Seriously. What?

My parents said hardly a word when I told them, just moved on past as if they hadn't heard me at all. My older brother, a doctor who almost never calls, rang me up. "I bet that's kind of hard," he said, and even though he was right and well intentioned, I heard myself tell him, No, it really isn't that hard. I don't mind painting. It's not that bad.

I'm sure he thought I was lying, and I might even have agreed, but there's more to it than that. Despite my frustration at once again pulling on crusty old paint clothes every morning, I also began to realize that in certain ways I *did* like painting better than the more esteemed occupations of teaching and editing—certain ways that actually mattered more the older I got.

For one thing, I noticed that my stomach didn't churn when I got out of bed in the morning to go painting the way it did before a day of performing my teacher act in front of thirty confrontational teenagers. And my muscles, while sore at first, soon got into the groove of manual labor again, leaving me feeling fit and lean as opposed to plopped and soft behind a desk. I appreciated more than ever the freedom of listening to my headphones and thinking my own thoughts all day, as opposed to battling high school students for control of the classroom or tackling the tedious task of reorganizing some professional writer's tossed-together manuscript.

I found a new appreciation for the buzz of a construction site, the united sense of purpose among the trades, the feel-good endorphins that come with immediate, tangible results. For me, trying to gauge progress among a group of surly teens was often a con, and the slow pace of book publishing dispensed mostly latent satisfaction months after the fact. But painting made the world a more beautiful place today—the indisputable evidence glowed right there in front of you. I no longer took that daily dose of achievement for granted. Not everybody gets one.

..

Unfortunately, just when I wanted to settle into a calm state of contentment about my situation, Larry got us involved in a construction disaster that ended up polluting a lot of my brain space. I watched powerlessly as Larry rode his business toward bankruptcy, and as Franklin came to distrust and then purposely abandon his own exceptional painting skills. And I became gripped by my hatred of the general contractor on the job, Karl, an obsessive-compulsive micromanager whose incompetence was matched only by his irrational fixation on pointless detail and his willingness to inflict financial ruin on any subcontractor who didn't comply.

I'm not a violent person, but as the weeks passed and the situation grew worse, I started fantasizing about revenge against Karl. I imagined myself breaking into his office with a baseball bat and destroying it. I daydreamed I was dressed in black, sneaking up on his house in the middle of the night to puncture the tires of his fancy pickup and rake my car keys deep into the truck's finish so the wounds could never be buffed out. I visualized a scene where I just plain smashed his face with my fist. I felt bizarre for having these thoughts, and I also resented the timing. Just when I wanted to focus on the positives of painting, the trade's alter ego took possession of my senses like a demon finally learning the breadth of its power. So you think you can glorify me as some sort of righteous, pleasurable profession? Foolish boy. I'll show you just how hateful I can be.

The job in question was a gut-and-remodel of a large home positioned perfectly on a prime point of land overlooking the waters of Puget Sound. The owners lived next door in a house they planned to sell as soon as the remodel was complete. Apparently, they had profited nicely after unloading some fast-food franchises in Arizona, then moved to this idyllic island to live in semi-retirement. They were relatively young and obviously business savvy, but they didn't have a clue about construction, and on the far-too-rare occasions when they toured the job and listened to Karl's lies, I would watch from the periphery in amazement and disgust. You poor people. Wake up, for Christ's sake, because you are taking it in the ass.

Word among the subs was that the cost estimate had started at $250,000. Costs then doubled, which isn't terribly unusual for a large remodel, but then, after months became a year and Karl's neurotic nitpicking only intensified, costs had almost doubled again. It didn't matter to Karl, whose contract was based on time and materials, but to the subs it was a profit eater and eventually an outright money loser.

The drywallers were the first to walk off. Their assignment had been to skim-coat the textured walls throughout the house and make them smooth wall. When several attempts to do this failed to pass Karl's inspection, the drywallers abandoned the job in furious frustration. Karl then shifted his own carpenters to the task, which demonstrated an amazing naïveté regarding the difficulty of doing good drywall work.

Day after day, week after week, these carpenters went room to room and wall to wall, mudding, sanding, sighing when Karl would shine his floodlight at all angles on the work and circle numerous infractions with his pencil; then they would mud, sand, and sigh again. They were excellent woodworkers who hated being forced to flail at another trade, but they worked directly for Karl so it wasn't really costing them anything but pride. They sympathized with subs like us and admitted Karl was a freak, but they had families to support, so onward they would trudge to the next room with their sanding poles, ready to be consumed by the fine white filth of a foreign profession, waiting for the day they could breathe sweet sawdust again.

Under the best circumstances, creating perfectly smooth drywall is difficult. It really just depends on how picky you want to be—if you shine a bright light sideways down it and stick your eyes within inches, of course you're going to see imperfections. And that's starting with fresh sheetrock, where only the joints and nail holes need to be mudded. A higher level of tolerance would be required if you wanted to skim-coat textured walls throughout a large house and turn it all into smooth wall. It's just not going to be perfect.

But Karl went the opposite direction. He fixated on the drywall past the point of comedy into absurdity. Admittedly, the carpenters did some shoddy work at first, but after the third or fourth pass things started to look pretty good. Certainly good enough for these customers, who were so absent they didn't even know that they were being charged time-and-materials for three well-paid carpenters to flounder away for four weeks with mud pans in their hands. All the customers knew was what Karl told them: the original drywall company had screwed up the job and now he had to fix it. The truth was that the original drywallers had picked Karl for a nut early on and bolted to minimize their losses.

The problem from a painting perspective started with the fact that several times Karl declared a room "ready" and ordered us to paint it, then afterward gave another inspection and ended up circling more spots right on top of our fresh coat. When Franklin presented him with add-on sheets for the extra time, Karl fumed that Larry had "fifty grand in the contract" and could spare a few extra hours. He signed the first couple add-ons, but after that refused to even look at them.

Early in the job, Larry—who rarely showed up on our job sites anyway but who made a special effort to stay away from this one—told Franklin to just do whatever Karl said and forget the add-ons. Despite the fifty grand he'd bid, he'd only gotten minimal money up front and, after a month, was another ten grand into it out of his own pocket, according to what he told Franklin. He needed to keep Karl happy long enough to collect that much, which was due him very soon according to the contract. Larry assured us that when he got that $10,000 check, we'd walk like the drywallers had.

Larry waited and waited, but the check didn't come; meanwhile, Franklin and I kept repainting rooms, sometimes three times—and if we complained, Karl would circle something invisible and tell us to redo the wall, just to put us in our place. Franklin burned with barely contained wrath every day, and eventually so did I. I couldn't help it—it just happened. In all my life I can't recall feeling as angry about anything. Paint on walls, that's it. Bloody paint on butchered walls.

Finally, another three grand into it, Larry pulled us off the job and went to Karl's office to demand his money. You want money? Karl said. Are you serious? If I pay you another ten grand on top of what I gave you up front, I will have paid you 30 percent of the contract. But the work is only 10 percent done, if that. Read the contract you signed—it specifically says I don't need to pay you any greater percentage of the total than the percentage of the job done, at any given point. And this job is far from being done, so you better get your damn painters back out there and get to work.

Of course, calculating the "percentage of the job done" was entirely at Karl's discretion. I'm sure Larry realized this with sickening remorse the day he left Karl's office unpaid, with only a vague promise that he would get some money in a couple weeks. He returned to the shop where Franklin and I were waiting and told us to go back the next day, and to keep going back. In fact, he was hiring a helper to come with us, because Karl had complained that there weren't enough painters on the job and we were slowing everybody else down.

"What?!" Franklin practically screamed. He fervently told Larry that the real problem, aside from the drywall, was the fact that the trim in every room was only half installed and not ready for painting due to Karl's fire-dousing method of pulling his crews off one thing and sticking them on another. But Larry just shook his head, face sagging with worry. We need to stick with it until I get some money, he said. We need to get something.

..

Franklin asked Larry every day for the next two weeks if the check had come. The answer was always no, so we kept going back, and somewhere along the way Franklin completed his transformation from conscientious craftsman to sub-conscious saboteur. He was so tight with repressed anger that his work became careless, which led Karl to complain even more, sometimes legitimately. But Franklin knew that Karl's compulsions were the core of the problem, and he refused to accept any responsibility. It culminated one day when he forgot to bring a fine-finish spray tip to spray oil enamel on some custom cabinetry.

"Oh well," he said, then blasted the woodwork with an old exterior latex tip and walked away. Later I shone a flood-light into the cabinets and inspected the thick runs. It was only a matter of time before Karl saw these—$5,000 worth of cabinets were fucked. Somebody would have to sand all those runs and repaint.

Franklin didn't care anymore. He only wanted to get away from this man who was deriding his skills and making him feel like the uneducated lowlife he desperately did not want to be—like he wasn't allowed to be good at anything. His taping grew lazy, resulting in ragged lines between colors. When I offered to touch them up with a brush, he pulled outright rank on me for the first time in two years and ordered me not to. "That asshole isn't paying us to do all this extra masking. This house was supposed to be four colors, that's it." He scowled viciously. "Fucking thief."

The "four colors" were at the heart of another major disagreement souring this job, the hyperbolic design scheme the owners had conceived. The upstairs alone had fifteen colors: every kid's bedroom had to be unique, with bright trim and subdued walls, capped by a white ceiling. The guest bedroom had two colors, the study two, the hallway two. All doorjambs between rooms had to be split colors to match the scheme. What this meant was a lot of extra time taping between colors, cleaning out the sprayer, scheduling time for colors to dry, just keeping all the damn colors straight in the first place. A few extra colors is no big deal, but fifteen in the upstairs was turning out to be a real pain.

But the original bid Larry submitted was based on Karl's instruction that the job would be two colors upstairs and two colors downstairs, four total. He told Larry to calculate it that way because as far as he knew that's all the customers wanted. Four colors.

Whether it was a genuine oversight or a deliberate swindle, it resulted in a significant miscalculation of the bid. But again, after the first few add-on sheets, Karl stopped signing them, complaining about what he thought were inflated hours. Franklin explained with increasing exasperation how much extra work it was to deal with the colors. He would show Karl our time sheets with the hours carefully documented. In response, Karl always diminished Franklin by asserting that he, Karl, knew how to paint too, at least enough to know that extra colors don't take that much extra time. Yes, they *do*, Franklin insisted over and over again. No, they *don't*, Karl would shoot back, and then he would turn and walk away, leaving Franklin riveted in disbelief.

Finally, the inevitable caving-in occurred. Larry hadn't been paid yet, and Franklin was under strict orders not to have any contact with Karl—I was assigned that responsibility—but one day we showed up to find our freshly sprayed trim in two bedrooms banged up by Karl's carpenters, who had been ordered back in to do a few more drywall fixes. So now, not only was the trim marred but two walls had to be re-done for a third time. The prospect was ruthlessly disheart-ening, making it seem as if ten weeks working on this hell job had not moved us one step toward completing it. It was Groundhog's Day for painters, and it was never going to end.

Right then Franklin decided it would end, at least for him. He grabbed an add-on sheet and filled it out, detailing the damage and estimating ten hours to fix it.

"That's good," I said. "Let me take it to him."

"Fuck that. I'm taking it to him."

"Franklin—"

I followed him out of the bedroom, down the stairs, and into the master bedroom, where Karl was standing with one of his carpenters discussing some intricately crafted cus-tom shelving.

"Sign this," Franklin said, pushing the clipboard forward.

Karl looked stunned for a moment, probably because Franklin hadn't spoken to him in weeks. But he quickly went on the offensive, grabbed the board, and inspected the add-on. Then he handed it back.

"I'm not signing this."

"Yes, you are."

"No, I'm not."

"Then we're stopping work immediately. We're done."

Karl issued a smirk. "Better talk to Larry first. The contract specifically prohibits you from stopping work, and I told Larry I'd sue him. Think he can afford to defend a lawsuit?"

"This is bullshit," Franklin said. "You don't want to pay us for the extra colors? Fine. But you are going to pay us for that room you fucked up." He shoved the clipboard forward again.

"Oh come on, those extra colors don't take that much time," Karl said, choosing to fight the more ambiguous battle—and the one he knew would more infuriate Franklin.

"Yes, they do," Franklin said, his voice rising.

"Oh come on, Franklin, I told you I know how to paint—"

"Karl, you don't know *shit* about painting."

"I know a lot about painting, Franklin," Karl said with a practiced sigh. "And I know that a few extra colors don't take that much time." Then, as if a switch had clicked erasing Franklin's existence, Karl turned away and started speaking calmly to the carpenter again.

Franklin shook his head once, then with enraged speed flung the clipboard like a Frisbee into the custom shelving. It banged against the wood, dinging and gouging, then rattled to a halt on the floor. "Fuck you, Karl. Just fuck you. You're a fucking asshole."

Karl spun around. "Franklin, *nobody* talks to me like that. Now get the hell off this job site." Spit flew from his lips as he yelled and pointed at the door.

"Fine," Franklin yelled back. He stalked out, and I followed him. When we reached the van in the driveway, he called Larry on the cell phone. He told him what had happened, then hung up. He stayed silent for a moment until I asked what Larry said.

"He said pack up our shit and get the fuck out of here."

And that is what we did.

..

I wish I could say that was the end of the hell job for me, but it wasn't. Eventually, Larry and Karl amended their contract by agreeing that we would take to completion everything we'd started—about two-thirds of the house's interior—and Karl would find another painter to finish the rest of the interior plus the exterior. They agreed to a dollar amount that was about $8,000 less than what Larry had into it, but at this point losing only $8,000 seemed like a gift from Heaven.

Larry sent me down alone for a couple of weeks to finish the work. Most of my time was spent with a brush in hand, repainting the lines between different colors, making them exceedingly straight to satisfy Karl's fetish. One day Larry actually did send Franklin with me, just to give Karl a poke. Franklin wasn't of much use, though, because brushing perfectly straight lines wasn't his forte. Still, I was glad to have him along for company. He seemed more relaxed than I would have expected, and we talked and joked around a lot because we missed working together.

Karl, upon seeing Franklin, beelined over and made a point of telling me how straight my lines looked—"a huge improvement"—then walked away. I thought Franklin would be angry, but instead he simply shrugged and admitted out loud that I was a better brusher than he was. The admission didn't cost him too much because he considered brushing the last resort of painting—real painters spray—but nonetheless, I felt proud that I could perform any aspect of the trade better than him. Even wimpy old brushing.

An outfit from Seattle had been brought in to finish the job, and Franklin was intensely curious about these new painters, so after lunch we cut through the taped-up plastic wall separating our side of the house from theirs and I introduced Franklin to Terry, foreman of the new crew. Terry was a nice guy and a good painter who had been union-trained down in the city, and so far his work had elicited many "ooohs" and "aaahs" from the homeowners when Karl gave them a tour. Through the plastic wall I had heard Karl tell the customers the job was "back on track" now that those "other" painters had quit. I bristled at being disparaged and imagined myself bursting through the plastic wall like a superhero and telling those people what was really going on, that this whole mess was Karl's fault, not ours. I wanted to tell them we *are* good painters—we are. I never thought I cared so much about that until somebody tried to take it away.

Terry's honeymoon with Karl soon ended, though, and during my last few days on the job I started to hear disagreements percolating through the plastic. Karl was nitpicking about the finish on the kitchen cabinets, and Terry was resisting. Terry started making more and more visits over to my side of the house to confirm that Karl was an honest-to-God nut. I was happy to concur.

I conveyed all this to Franklin one day when I stopped by his trailer house to pick up some equipment. He listened eagerly, relieved to find out Terry wasn't such a great painter after all. He laughed hard when I told him the real kicker: now a *third* painting company was being hired to finish the job. Terry's outfit had done exactly what we did—cut it off and quit.

"That's hilarious," Franklin said, shaking his head. "Three painting companies on one job. Who knows, maybe they'll need four before they're done. Don't forget they're going to build a garage and a guest house."

"Yeah, that's right. They'll probably need at least five to get it all done."

We laughed together and walked over to Larry's paint van, which was parked at Franklin's because Larry let him drive it for personal use, a nice perk that saved Franklin some gas money.

"Larry said he wants his van back," Franklin informed me as I grabbed some gear out. "He wants me to leave it at the shop every night." It wasn't unreasonable for Larry to want his company van back, but Franklin sounded worried, as if without that connection his future was less certain. He sensed that the trauma of the hell job had cracked his and Larry's ten-year relationship, and now they were starting to separate.

Franklin's house sat on three acres, and the grounds were meticulously kept, as if to defy the stereotypical image of a junk-laden trailer-house yard. I'd never been there so Franklin gave me a tour, showing me the greenhouse he'd built, a hole he'd dug for a pond, and the woods out back where he let people hunt deer, adding that I was welcome to as well. He also introduced me to his seven-year-old daughter, who played in the yard while we talked.

Every so often, a plane from the nearby naval air station would fly over, an EA-6B Prowler the military depended on to jam enemy radar in places like Iraq and Afghanistan. The planes were low to the ground, going in for a landing, seeming close enough to plink with a BB gun. The powerful roar of the jets—so loud and so near—jarred me. I remembered how Franklin had said he lived "underneath the planes" on the first day we worked together three years ago.

His daughter didn't look up from her play as the planes flew over, and Franklin spoke right through the black noise as if it were no big deal. But I saw a shadow of embarrassment cross his face as if he was imagining what I must see: a painter living in a trailer in a war zone. I wanted to tell him what I really saw—a single dad doing everything for his daughter—but instead I just ignored the planes too. That's what Franklin wanted me to do, and he was my boss.

..

Speaking of daughters, my wife and I welcomed our own daughter that winter of the hell job. Larry and Franklin were my male confidants throughout the whole experience, and I was glad to have them because childbirth is a nervous time. Larry had one daughter who was grown, so he was the wise old dad, responding to my complaint about sleepless nights by saying, "It never ends." Franklin, asserting his position of moderate experience, warned me that the worst thing about having a daughter was brushing her tangled hair every morning. Seriously, he said, it's the hardest thing I do all day. These conversations about fatherhood helped ease the torment of the hell job for all of us that winter. It was impossible to talk about our daughters without receiving a strong dose of perspective.

When summer came it brought some luck, and I was rehired as a teacher at the high school for the upcoming year. Once again I bid good-bye to Franklin and Larry in the driveway of the shop, but this time we all agreed I'd be back. Somehow, some way, I'd be back.

I never did go back to Larry, though, even when I got laid off from teaching again the following spring. Instead, I decided to stir up some of my former editing contacts and see if I could make it as a freelancer. This would not have been an option if my wife didn't earn a decent salary from her teaching job, but she did, so I went for it. I worked from home and did some extra parenting because my schedule was flexible.

I didn't get out much, though, and I didn't see Franklin for about a year. I was surprised one day when the phone rang and it was him. He sounded tense, and after a brief greeting he got to the point. "Hey, did you tell Larry I'm a shitty painter?"

"What?" That was about the last thing I expected him to say. "Franklin, come on. Why would I say you're a shitty painter? You're a great painter."

He exhaled a tight breath. "Larry said that you said I was a shitty painter. But I didn't believe him. I didn't think you would ever say that."

"Of course I would never say that. Give me a break."

"Yeah, that's what I thought." Then he told me the story of how his worst fear had finally come true: one of the painters Larry hired was a decent hand, and eventually he got his brother on the crew, and the two of them ganged up on Franklin and started trashing him behind his back to Larry. Larry was ready to buy in this time, with his view of Franklin forever stained by the hell job no matter whose fault it was, and one day he tried to demote Franklin from crew leader to crew member. That was the end of their eleven years together.

"I told him not to listen to those guys," Franklin said. "I told him they're fucking druggies and liars, because they are. That's when he said that you said the same thing—that I'm a shitty painter, and that I screwed everything up on that remodel job."

"Franklin, there's no way." I felt the futility that comes with combating the most indefatigable of enemies: a lie. Larry had needed to better arm his argument, and I was the spear with the most credibility flung to wound Franklin deeply.

"Yeah, that's what I told him," he said. "I just wanted to hear you say it."

"Seriously, I would never talk behind your back like that, or say you're a shitty painter. I think you're a great painter."

"Yeah, I know."

The conversation eased. He told me he'd found a job working full time for a local builder who specialized in high-end custom homes—a builder who formerly gave the contracts to Larry. Franklin was now doing all the guy's painting, doing it well, doing it fast, and alleviating for the builder one of the hugest potential headaches on any high-end custom home: getting a top-quality paint job that does justice to the house's other custom features and fineries. And the builder was getting it at a discount rate because there was no middle-man painting contractor like Larry to pay—just Franklin, who could do the whole damn thing by himself.

"It sounds like everything worked out after all," I said. "I bet that pisses Larry off that you took all that work from him."

"Yeah," he said with a deep sigh, "but it doesn't matter anyway. I'm so sick of painting, it just depresses me anymore. I wish I could do something else." He trailed off, and I sensed he was thinking about me, reclining at a desk all day, relying on my education to make me money. How nice that must have sounded to him. How impossible to attain.

..

About a year later I left a message on Franklin's voice mail saying I was getting ready to spray my kitchen cabinets and I would like him to stop by and give me some pointers. Six months later he called back.

"Sorry it took so long."

"That's okay."

"You probably painted those cabinets by now."

"I haven't, actually."

"Oh, good. I'll stop by this week and look them over. Hey, guess what?" Right then I realized he hadn't called about the cabinets. Instead, he told me that he'd gotten so fed up with painting that he just quit one day with no advance warning, even in his own mind. He just couldn't take another day of it. The home builder, threatened with the loss of his own private money-printing machine, freaked out and made Franklin an offer he couldn't refuse: $55,000 a year, paid time off, and health insurance. "He also said I could join his 401(k)," Franklin added. I could hear the pride in his voice, his amazement at the sudden realization of his own worth.

"That's awesome, Franklin."

"You know," he said, "I have to admit that painting seems much better now. I don't hate it anymore." We both laughed. "But I'm serious," he said. "I don't mind painting nearly as much as I used to. It's weird."

"Cool," was all I could think to say.

"So how's your stuff going?" he asked, wanting to hear from my own lips how much he had the college boy beat by.

"Great," I said, leaving out a few details. I had made $18,000 my first year as a freelancer, but that wasn't the bad news. The bad news was that I had a folder on my desk containing filled-out paperwork to get a painting contractor's license from the State of Washington, because the publishing company I did most of my freelancing for had just informed me they were bringing the work in-house and my services would no longer be required. Other freelance jobs were proving hard to come by, so I'd already painted two houses for cash and was looking for more. At forty-one years old I was gearing up, mind and body, to get back in the business. It was not a transition I was looking forward to from any angle.

"Good," he said, and I was glad he didn't pursue it. He'd see me on the painter circuit soon enough anyway, and there would be plenty of time to explain.

..

I never went back. In the end, everything worked out for me too. First, my wife and I welcomed another darling baby girl into our lives, and all went well with that. Then, quite unexpectedly, the publishing company offered me a full-time position working from home, preventing me from ever having to submit that contractor's application. This gig allowed a subsequent move for our family back to Montana, which is where my wife and I had decided we wanted to live. Of course, my salary still can't compare to Franklin's, but I don't begrudge him the money as I sit gratefully at my desk, editing and e-mailing instead of lifting ladders and taking in toxins. I know how hard it is out there. I know painting is anything but simple.

acknowledgments

I would like to thank everybody who has supported my writing over the years by publishing my work or offering words of encouragement. This starts with my parents, who always thought my sporadic publications were big deals, and especially my mom, a voracious reader who never passes up a chance to tell me how much she likes my stories and how she reads them over again. Mom and Dad, I don't take your support for granted just because you are my parents. I love you.

Thanks also to my siblings for reading my stories over the years and being supportive.

I've had some teachers who encouraged my literary efforts and gave me good advice. Chronologically, I would like to thank Joan Schultz, Michael Herzig, Jesse Bier, Earl Ganz, William Kittredge, Carol Van Valkenburg, and, especially, Sharon Barrett—short story writer, journalist, book critic, teacher, and friend—whose simple but powerful words of encouragement helped provide me with motivation for more than twenty years.

I would also like to express my appreciation to some magazine and newspaper editors who gave encouragement and published my work: George Bracksieck, Marjorie McCloy, DeAnne Musolf, Dougald MacDonald, David Harrower, Ross Prather, Mike Kord, Butch Larcomb, Peggy O'Neill, and others whose names I can't recall but who played an important role in getting my stories published. The positive attention you paid to my work helped energize me through the years.

I'd also like to thank Dottie Read and the Whidbey Island Writer's Association. This book had its genesis in an essay called "On Painting" that won an award at WIWA's conference in 2005. That award, and the positive reactions I got from people as we did readings at libraries around the island, convinced me that painting was a topic worthy of further exploration.

Special thanks to everybody who helped me put together the book: My wife, Claire, who waded through early drafts; Allen Jones for his developmental editing comments; Shana Harrington for copyediting; Ann Seifert for proofreading; Jeff Wincapaw for the cover and interior designs; Dana Kim-Wincapaw for the page layout; and Luke Duran, graphic designer, for his website work. None of you charged me anything close to what your skills are worth, and I will always be grateful for your help.

Also, thanks to all my colleagues in book publishing for helping me learn the skills of that trade.

Finally, I would like to express my appreciation to all the painters I've worked with over the years. I changed your names to protect your privacy, but the real credit for these stories belongs to you. You made a hard job tolerable, sometimes even enjoyable, and I thank you.

about the author

In addition to having been a professional painter for fifteen years, **John Burbidge** is a writer whose award-winning stories have appeared in a variety of magazines, newspapers, and anthologies. He lives in Helena, Montana, with his wife and two daughters. Read more of his stories at www.johnburbidge.com.

Also visit his website www.howtopaintahouseright.com, where you'll find a complete series of videos John created to help you paint your house—right!

Getting ready to paint your house?

Go to www.howtopaintahouseright.com to view a complete series of videos John Burbidge has created to help you paint your house—**right**!

CPSIA information can be obtained at www.ICGtesting.com
Printed in the USA
BVOW032306300513

322089BV00001B/4/P